First Supplement to 'THE TOWN REEVES OF BUNGAY' (2nd Edition: 1725 – 2007) by JOHN HARRIS,   ROSELAND PUBLISHING,   ISBN : 978-0-948973-01-7

MARTIN EVANS
Town Reeve
2007-08

2007-08
MARTIN EVANS, B.Sc.

He was born on 26 November 1940 at Lemsford, Hertfordshire, and educated at St. Albans School and London University, where he gained an Honours Special degree in zoology in 1961, specialising in entomology.

The following year, Mr. Evans joined the Cooper Technical Bureau, Berkhamsted, as an advisory entomologist; this later became the Wellcome Foundation. He travelled throughout the tropics, primarily concerned with mosquito and tsetse fly control. In 1966 he married Miss Pauline Booth and they have a daughter and a son.

Mr. Evans was President of the British Pest Control Association for two years from 1978 and of the European Federation of Pest Control Associations from 1981 to 1982. He retired from the group in 1998 as Regional Manager (Africa and Asia) and as a Director of their South African company.

Mr. & Mrs. Evans moved to Bungay in 1977, living in the old cottage on the Drift, Outney Road, owned by John Barber Scott (six times Town Reeve). Mr. Evans was Chairman of the Bungay Society for three years from 2002, and in 2008 became Chairman of the Friends of St. Mary's Priory Church and President of Bungay Rotary Club. He was elected a Town Councillor in 2003, serving as Mayor from 2006 to 2007.

Appointed to the Town Trust as a Foundation Feoffee in 2005, Mr. Evans became Town Reeve in December 2007. During his term of office he staged 'Bigod's Music in the Castle Keep' during the Bungay Festival and, with his wife, a garden party exhibiting the works of art of his late father, the *Prix de Rome* sculptor, David Evans. Funds raised during the year were to be donated to various Bungay organisations.

Obit. Addenda: -
(p.67) Mr. Duhy died on 27 April 2008.
(p.85) Mrs. Belcher died on 30 May 2008.

Price 50p

Second Supplement to 'THE TOWN REEVES OF BUNGAY' (2nd Edition: 1725-2007)
by John Harris,   ROSELAND PUBLISHING,   ISBN: 978-0-948973-01-7

CHRISTOPHER HAND
Town Reeve
2008-09

2008-09
Professor CHRISTOPHER HILLARY HAND, MA MSc MB BChir FRCP FRCGP

A distant relative of Sir William Hillary, the founder of the Royal Lifeboat Institution, he was born on 5 November 1946 at the Middlesex Hospital, London, and educated at St. Edward's School, Oxford. He studied medicine at Clare College, Cambridge, where he achieved a scholarship, and at the Middlesex Hospital, London, where he met his wife, Lesley, who was a night sister. They were married in 1972 and have two sons and a daughter. He also worked at Cheltenham, Oxford, Ipswich (where his father was a surgeon), and Hammersmith Hospital, but became a trainee general practitioner in Ipswich after deciding against a career in hospital medicine.

Dr. Hand moved to Bungay in 1976 to join the practice of Dr. Charles Maidment (Town Reeve 1971-72). The following year this practice joined Dr. Wyndham Jordan (Town Reeve 1973-74) and Dr. Brian Goss to form the first combined general practice in Bungay which was based at the Beeches. In 2001 and 2002 he led the team which designed and built the Bungay Medical Centre at St. John's Road - this is now run as a charitable trust, thanks to a substantial donation from Miss Kathleen Bowerbank, and is now combined with the Scott Charity.

In 2002 Dr. Hand was awarded the British Medical Association Sir James Cameron Award for services to general practice. In 2005 he was conferred with the honorary title of Professor by the University of East Anglia in recognition of his help in setting up the medical school there. He started this work in 2002 and is now one of the Deputy Directors.

Dr. Hand was appointed to the Town Trust as a Foundation Feoffee in 1982. He was the Founder Chairman of the Black Dog Running Club, which established the Bungay Marathon in the same year; he ran several times in the half-marathon event. He has sung tenor with his Cambridge College Choral Society, the Bach Choir in London, Beccles Choral Society, the Keswick Hall Choir in Norwich, and with the male voice octet Arbutus until it disbanded in 2006. For some years he has performed the traditional Town Song at Bungay Town Dinner.

During his year of office as Town Reeve, Professor Hand has raised funds for the R.N.L.I. and All Hallows Hospital, Ditchingham, by holding a dinner at the Fisher Theatre and a coffee morning at the Pines.

Erratum:-
First Supplement to 2nd Edition, line 12:-
For '1977' read '1997'.   Price 50p

Third Supplement to 'THE TOWN REEVES OF BUNGAY' (2nd Edition 1725-2007) by JOHN HARRIS,   ROSELAND PUBLISHING,   ISBN: 978-948973-01-7

JOHN GROOM
Town Reeve
2009-10

2009-10
JOHN WILLIAM GROOM

He was born on 26 March 1948 at Ipswich, and educated at the Primary and Secondary Schools at Bramford. Leaving school at 15, he started work for Ipswich Co-op as a trainee butcher, and has remained in the same trade ever since. In 1983, he moved to Bungay and bought his butchery business in Wingfield Street.

Mr. Groom, who has a daughter from a previous marriage, in 2009 married his partner of twelve years, Jayne Niblett, while in office as Mayor. Together, they have built up a flourishing outside catering business.

Mr. Groom was elected to Bungay Town Council and Waveney District Council in 2000, and served as Mayor for two consecutive years from 2007. He was appointed as a Foundation Feoffee in 2004, and became Town Reeve in 2009. He is also Chairman of Planning with Waveney District Council, and a member and keen supporter of many organisations within the town; he was President of Bungay Rotary Club in 1998.

During his year of office as Town Reeve, Mr. Groom revived the Town Reeve's Ball and raised over £5,000 for the East Anglian Air Ambulance and All Hallows Hospital, Ditchingham. Over the years, he has helped and supported Bungay Guides to achieve the building of a new Guide Hut.

Obit.Addendum:-
(p.86) Mr. Jervis died on 17 July 2010.   Price 50p

THE TOWN REEVES
OF BUNGAY
2nd Edition: 1725-2007

THOMAS MANNING
Town Reeve
**1757-58, 1768-69, 1776-77,
1783-84 & 1784-85**

The earliest known portrait of a Town Reeve of Bungay.

THE TOWN REEVES OF BUNGAY

2nd Edition: 1725-2007

A study of a unique and ancient office
and those who have occupied it
by

JOHN HARRIS

ROSELAND PUBLISHING
in association with

MORROW & CO.
PUBLISHERS
BUNGAY, SUFFOLK
2007

*I dedicate this book
to all members of my family,
past and present,
who have loved Bungay –
and the second edition
to the memory of
Rosalind M., Hugh C. and Cicely S.*

© JOHN HARRIS, 1986 & 2007

Harris, John Rowland, 1942 Dec. 16 -

The Town Reeves of Bungay:
a study of a unique and ancient office and those who have occupied it.
(2nd Edition: 1725-2007).

British Library Cataloguing in Publication Data: –

A catalogue record for this book is available from the British Library.

ISBN 978-0-948973-01-7

Printed by the Witley Press Ltd., Hunstanton, Norfolk.

First Edition (1725-1986) published 1986

Second Edition (1725-2007) published 2007

Front Cover:
The Town Reeve's Chain of Office and
Bungay Scenes (clockwise from top left):-
The Castle, Castle Hills, the Butter Cross,
Holy Trinity Church, Emmanuel Church
(formerly Bungay Congregational Church),
the Town Sign, the River Waveney at the Common,
St. Mary's Church, Bungay Primary School,
the Market Place.

FOREWORD
to the Second Edition
by
THE TOWN REEVE OF BUNGAY
(Mrs. Maureen Davies)

It is an extraordinary honour to be Town Reeve of Bungay and a considerable additional privilege to be asked to write the foreword to this second edition of John Harris's history of the Reeves. Bungay is fortunate to have someone like John who is prepared to invest the time and thought necessary to produce such a book and the social conscience which inspires him to keep Bungay's history alive in this way.

I was not living in Bungay when the first edition was published: my own copy was bought second-hand some years ago. When I first read it I never imagined that I might ever feature in the next edition as the twelfth of Bungay's female Reeves.

Intriguingly, however, I am continuing a tradition associated with my home. Rose Hall has been occupied by past Town Reeves on at least fifteen occasions, although some of these past Reeves held the office many times – Richard Nelson six times and his nephew Nelson Burtsal eight times in the 18th and early 19th centuries. The last holder of the office who lived in the house was Charles Parry-Crooke who was Reeve in 1934 and lived in Bungay until 1948. There must still be some people in Bungay who remember him.

I congratulate the author and trust that this new version of his book will enjoy as much success as the first one did and that it will encourage the Town of Bungay to take continued pride in its Town Trust, Feoffees and Town Reeve.

MAUREEN DAVIES
Town Reeve

April 2007

AUTHOR'S INTRODUCTION
TO THE SECOND EDITION

I was delighted with – if somewhat amazed by – the measure of success and apparent popularity enjoyed by the first edition of my book, even to the extent that I have discovered it is now offered on the Internet as a 'colletor's item', at more than six times the original asking price! However, after more than two decades, and now well into a new century, I have been persuaded by the Town Trust that a second edition is now indicated, and hope not only that the present volume will appeal to a new generation of readers, but that those who have already studied the first edition will enjoy the new pages, presenting sixteen new Town Reeves (plus five repeat terms) and containing many photographs of former incumbents which have come to light in the intervening years.

I have left my original introduction intact without alteration, but readers should be aware that it was written twenty-one years ago, and that inevitably the wind of change has blown around Bungay, as elsewhere, in the meantime. The number of lady Reeves has doubled to a round dozen, and all three of my erstwhile main mentors have sadly died, and are greatly missed. The Chairman of Bungay Town Council is now dignified with the title of Mayor, but the ancient office of Town Reeve retains all of its historic prestige, and its uniqueness remains unchallenged.

I am grateful to the present Town Reeve, Mrs. Maureen Davies, for help, encouragement and generous hospitality, and to her immediate predecessor, Mrs. Mary Kent, for her continuing interest and support. I also wish to thank Messrs. Chris Reeve, Martin Evans and Frank Honeywood for help with photographic research and reproduction, and all former Reeves still living and the relatives of many now sadly deceased for information which has enabled me to update several entries.

It is always a delight to travel from one end of Norfolk to the other, and just across the Suffolk border, to visit my home town and maintain a keen interest in its civic affairs. In particular I have for several years now enjoyed attending the Town Dinner, at which I have twice had the honour of being a guest speaker. Revising my book has been a total pleasure, and by making this further contribution to Bungay's documented history, I trust that I am able to go some way towards thanking the town and its people for the many happy memories of my childhood, and for the warm welcome which I, along with so many others, regularly experience when coming 'home'.

JOHN HARRIS

August 2007

FOREWORD
to the First Edition
by
THE TOWN REEVE OF BUNGAY, 1985-86
(Mrs. Cicely Smith)

I am sure that all Town Reeves have felt, as I have, great pride and honour at following in the footsteps of the many illustrious holders of an office cloaked in such tradition and history and it is high time a survey of that office and its incumbents should be carried out. It was thus with particular pleasure that I learned that John Harris had chosen my year of office to bring to fruition a project which I know he has had in mind for some ten years, first because of the necessity to fill a gap in the Bungay archives and secondly because John is someone whom I have known all his life. I remember from our youth that John has always had a great interest in the office of Town Reeve and indeed never more so than when his uncle, Mr. Cecil Harris, was appointed in 1962. John has spent a great deal of time researching his book and it has become quite fascinating as he has gradually uncovered many unknown facts - far more than he has been able to include in this volume. I hope that his book will do much to encourage a continuing interest in the Town Trust and the ancient and historic office of Town Reeve.

CICELY SMITH
Town Reeve

September 1986

IN MEMORIAM
Mrs. CICELY SMITH
Town Reeve, 1985-86

Cicely died on 11 December 1991, only a few days after I had visited her in Ditchingham Hospital. Her illness had prevented her from being pesent at the Town Dinner the previous evening, but she was as always keen to hear news of the event, and I was able to give her a copy of the first supplement to my book, which she looked forward to reading.

Cicely's death followed barely a year after that of Mrs. Rosalind Messenger – I little thought that we should lose both these outstanding ladies within such a comparatively short time of the publication of my book, with which they both gave me much help, sound advice and greatly valued encouragement.

Cicely was extremely patient and forebearing in allowing me to "impose" my project on virtually the whole of her year in office, but I was delighted to have achieved my ambition to write the book while she was Town Reeve.

Cicely's husband, Harry, and her fellow Feoffees on Bungay Town Trust have been kind enough to agree that my book should now stand as a permanent tribute to her term of office as Town Reeve, and to the memory of a lifelong friend whom I, along with very many others, will always hold in high esteem and special affection.

JOHN HARRIS

November 1995

AUTHOR'S INTRODUCTION AND ACKNOWLEDGEMENTS

"Who's the new Town Reeve?" is a question which has found its way onto the lips of Bungayans every December, certainly for as long as I can remember. Indeed, the annual revelation of the identity of each successive occupant of this unique and ancient office has become one of the most firmly-established and fascinating traditions of my home town. The exact origins of the office of Town Reeve of Bungay are likely to remain shrouded in mystery for all time, and history also appears unwilling to yield up the identity of the early chief citizens of the town. However, a complete list of Reeves dating from 1725 is extant, and the current work seeks to bring together some of the documentary evidence of the survival and continuity of the office into modern times.

While, inevitably, some of the history of Bungay - the town, its buildings and traditions - unfolds in these pages, this book purports to be essentially a document of human interest, highlighting the lives and achievements of the men - and six women - who have occupied the office of Town Reeve over the last two and a half centuries. From the august figures of the past, through the distinguished presences of which one was aware in one's childhood and youth, to today's incumbent - a friend I have known all my life - I have tried to give an insight into many diverse characters, and to chronicle some of the more notable events which have taken place during their various terms of office.

It seemed, however, that the present book would be incomplete without a summary of the office itself, and I have accordingly included a brief account of its historic traditions and routine duties as well as of the more lustrous activities of those who find the honour thrust upon them in the latter years of the twentieth century.

While researching and preparing my book, I have received much help and co-operation from the Town Reeve, Mrs. Cicely Smith, from all of her predecessors still living, and from the relatives of many other former occupants of the office. The Senior Feoffee, Mrs. Rosalind Messenger, has given me valued advice and encouragement, and I am indeed indebted for particular help and specific guidance with some of the biographies to Dr. Hugh Cane, whose knowledge of matters Bungayan is set to become as legendary as that of his late father! To all the aforementioned, and to many other friends, I wish to express my grateful thanks, and I offer the 1986 publication of the result of our combined efforts as a particular tribute to Dr. Cane's devotion to Bungay, and to Mrs. Messenger's 'golden' anniversary as a member of the Town Trust, as well as to Mrs. Smith's year of office.

I have tried to leave no stone unturned in my quest to present the definitive work on my chosen subject. Maybe some future historian, taking the story onwards, may expand any part of my narrative with details which may still be brought to light regarding earlier years. In the meantime, and for my part, I have been privileged to make this contribution to the documented history of the town to which I am indebted for a large part of my upbringing and education, and for which I - along with countless others - retain a very special affection.

JOHN HARRIS

September 1986

THE OFFICE OF
TOWN REEVE OF BUNGAY

The designation 'Town Reeve' is the term by which modern times have known the important office, steeped in history since its inception in Anglo-Saxon times, of 'tun-gerefa'. Possibly more than a thousand years ago this would have been the man appointed by his contemporaries, as a kind of magistrate, to administer and control a 'tun' or small township. Other forms of 'gerefa' have survived into modern times, such as Port Reeves, Fen Reeves and Shire Reeves (the 'sheriffs' of today's parlance), but, despite repeated claims from other places where admittedly similar titles survive, the town of Bungay, nestling in a loop of the River Waveney on the Suffolk side of the border with Norfolk, remains proud in the belief that it is the only place in England to boast a Town Reeve as such.

Nowadays, the Town Reeve presides over the Bungay Town Trust, a benevolent and charitable institution dating possibly from the sixteenth century. This survives as a body of 'Feoffees', appointed as trustees of various lands and properties conveyed to the town and people of Bungay over the years. The Town Reeve would almost certainly have become associated with the Town Trust, being referred to in some documents as the 'Primer Feoffee'.

The earliest known Deed of Feoffment is dated 1639; new deeds have periodically been prepared, allowing for the appointment of twenty-four Feoffees - until very recent years, since when, by order of the Charity Commissioners, the number has been increased to thirty-four, ten of whom are elected by the Town Council. Being traditionally a self-perpetuating body, the Trust has the power to appoint in the place of members who die, or occasionally resign, other prominent, influential and suitable citizens. It does seem, however, that appointments to vacancies on the Town Trust have not always been made as assiduously as is the case today. Researches have indicated, in fact, that in the early nineteenth century its numbers were reduced to two, who served alternately as Town Reeve for some years - and that on the death of his fellow Feoffee, John Cooper (Senior) ran the town's affairs single-handed until 1809, when he appointed as many as forty-two others to assist him! Not all of these were to serve as Town Reeve.

The first Town Reeve known by name is William Brooke, mentioned in St. Mary's Churchwardens' Book in 1536, and it is a matter for reasonable conjecture that the names of Throckmorton, Popeson, Wingfield, and others famed in the chronicles of Bungay, would have figured among those serving the office in earlier centuries. A series of Town Reeves' Books is known to have been kept since 1548; however, the first has sadly disappeared without trace, so that a full and consecutive list is only available from the second volume, beginning in 1725. In earlier times, the comparatively few Feoffees would serve as Town Reeve on numerous occasions, usually in strict rotation; the tradition of the incumbent's right to choose his or her own successor, to be revealed only on the evening of the Annual Town Meeting, seems to have evolved in the early years of the 20th Century.

The said Annual Town Meeting is held on the evening of the first Tuesday in

December, formerly at the King's Head, then at the Centenary Rooms, and nowadays at the Chaucer Institute, following some years at the Community Centre. Following brief reports and presentation of Town Trust accounts, the Town Reeve reviews the year of office now closing, and proceeds to the main business - and highlight - of the evening, the naming of his or her successor. Bungay's new chief citizen, in accepting office, and having been duly invested with the gown and chain of office, outlines his or her programme, theme or intentions for the year ahead, and at the close of the meeting, in accordance with ancient tradition, those present are invited to sign the massive book containing the town accounts. Also traditionally, the new Town Reeve's first duty has been to proceed to one of the town's hostelries to offer liquid refreshment to the bellringers who have been busy in the church tower ringing in the new appointment. In former days, the Town Band would play in the streets and outside the new Town Reeve's home!

Tradition further demands that during the first month in office the Town Reeve on Christmas Day visits the occupants of the town's two groups of almshouses, and the patients at All Hallows Hospital, Ditchingham, in which the Town Trust has long had an interest. Usually in January, the first of some four meetings during the year is held, with the Town Reeve and Feoffees planning the expenditure of the now somewhat diminished income of the town purse. The upkeep and repair of the Butter Cross and the future of the Castle have been perennially on the agenda; matters for attention in former years included care of the poor, education of the young, water, fire and street-lighting services, watchmen, scavenging, and bellringing.

Among the more glamorous engagements of the Town Reeve are the annual Harvest Festival Service at Bury St. Edmunds for all the civic dignitaries of Suffolk, and the annual Remembrance Sunday Service, when a wreath is laid at the War Memorial. A Town Reeve's Ball and varying kinds of concert are among the other events which have been organized, the proceeds generally going to the Town Trust for its charitable works. Some of the town's organizations invite the Reeve to be their Honorary President for the duration of the term of office, and fêtes, etc., are opened, commemorative plaques unveiled, centenarians visited, with the Town Reeve attending, in official capacity, any major event held in Bungay. It has fallen to the lot of the Town Reeve to read the Proclamation of the Accession of each new Sovereign, and loyal greetings have been addressed at times of Royal celebration and on other occasions of national moment.

The glorious culmination of the year of office comes with the Town Dinner. This major event, known to have been held from 1725, and possibly even earlier, at the annual 'reckoning', or audit of the town accounts, was originally a period of merriment and cheer lasting from 3 p.m. onwards! Having been allowed to lapse in 1873, it was sixty years later revived, and is now held on the Friday evening preceeding the Town Meeting, its various homes having been the King's Head Hotel, the Secondary Modern School, and latterly the Community Centre and Bungay High School. The Town Reeve presides over an elegant company, and will have been responsible for the choice of principal guest speakers, who traditionally have been folk connected with his or her own calling or profession. Loyal and other toasts are drunk, there is dancing, and eagerly awaited annually is the singing, with additional topical verses, of the song 'Old Bungay', originally sung at Bungay Theatre in 1816. One could, in fact, do far worse, before proceeding to list and account for those who have held the office of Town Reeve of Bungay, than to conclude this general summary of the historic office itself by reiterating that song's famous chorus, being words in praise of the town of which, by common consent dating back into the mists of time, the Town Reeve is the civic and social head:

> 'Of all the fam'd towns this famed Island can boast,
> Where's the like of old Bungay? Search through the whole host!
> Then of all places, this is the place of renown:
> Oh! What a place is Old Bungay!
> Old Bungay's a wonderful Town!'

THE TOWN REEVE

Year	Name	Year	Name
1725-26	James King	1796-97	Nelson Burtsal
1726-27	Richard Nelson	1797-98	Dixon Gamble
1727-28	John King	1798-99	John Cooper
1728-29	Joshua Nelson	1799-1800	Nelson Burtsal
1729-30	John Dalling (Jnr.)	1800-01	John Cooper
1730-31	John Dalling (Snr.)	1801-02	Nelson Burtsal
1731-32	John Hemblen	1802-03	John Cooper
1732-33	John Botwright	1803-04	Nelson Burtsal
1733-34	John Dalling	1804-05	John Cooper
1734-35	Thomas Walker	1805-06	Nelson Burtsal
1735-36	Henry Williams	1806-07	John Cooper
1736-37	Richard Nelson	1807-08	John Cooper
1737-38	John Dalling	1808-09	John Cooper
1738-39	Thomas Walker	1809-10	John Cooper
1739-40	Richard Nelson	1810-11	John Cooper
1740-41	John King	1811-12	Matthias Kerrison
1741-42	Henry Williams	1812-13	Wolfran Lewis
1742-43	John Dalling	1813-14	John Scott
1743-44	Thomas Walker	1814-15	John Scott
1744-45	Richard Nelson	1815-16	John Scott
1745-46	Robert Clarke	1816-17	John Scott
1746-47	Henry Williams	1817-18	John Scott
1747-48	Richard Nelson	1818-19	Matthew Brettingham Kingsbury
1748-49	Thomas Walker	1819-20	Richard Mann (Snr.)
1749-50	Henry Williams	1820-21	William Denny
1750-51	Richard Nelson	1821-22	Matthias Abel
1751-52	Thomas Walker	1822-23	Robert Burtsal
1752-53	Henry Williams	1823-24	Robert Camell
1753-54	Richard Nelson	1824-25	John Brettell
1754-55	John Meen	1825-26	James Sheppard
1755-56	John Van Kamp	1826-27	John Cooper (Jnr.)
1756-57	Edward Cooper	1827-28	Edward Kerrison
1757-58	Thomas Manning	1828-29	John Barber Scott
1758-59	Robert Williams	1829-30	Pearse Walker
1759-60	William Lamb	1830-31	William Mann
1760-61	Thomas Plowman	1831-32	Robert Aggas Burtsal
1761-62	Thomas Prentice	1832-33	John Scott
1762-63	Isaac Reeve	1833-34	Matthew Brettingham Kingsbury
1763-64	William Pell	1834-35	Robert Butcher
1764-65	Samuel Botwright	1835-36	Richard Mann (Snr.)
1765-66	Dixon Gamble	1836-37	William Denny
1766-67	John Meen	1837-38	Robert Burtsal (Snr.)
1767-68	John Van Kamp	1838-39	John Brettell
1768-69	Thomas Manning	1839-40	John Brettell
1769-70	Thomas Plowman	1840-41	Nelson Burtsal
1770-71	William Pell	1841-42	John Barber Scott
1771-72	Samuel Botwright	1842-43	Pearse Walker
1772-73	Dixon Gamble	1843-44	Richard Mann (Jnr.)
1773-74	Nelson Burtsal	1844-45	William Mann
1774-75	John Cooper	1845-46	Robert Burtsal
1775-76	John Van Kamp	1846-47	William Denny & John Barber Scott
1776-77	Thomas Manning	1847-48	John Barber Scott
1777-78	William Pell	1848-49	Pearse Walker
1778-79	Samuel Botwright	1849-50	Richard Mann
1779-80	Dixon Gamble	1850-51	William Mann
1780-81	Nelson Burtsal	1851-52	Robert Burtsal
1781-82	John Williams Plowman	1852-53	John Barber Scott
1782-83	John Van Kamp	1853-54	Pearse Walker
1783-84	Thomas Manning	1854-55	Richard Mann
1784-85	Thomas Manning	1855-56	William Mann
1785-86	Dixon Gamble	1856-57	John Barber Scott
1786-87	Nelson Burtsal	1857-58	Pearse Walker
1787-88	John Cooper	1858-59	Richard Mann
1788-89	John Williams Plowman	1859-60	William Mann
1789-90	John Van Kamp	1860-61	John Mann
1790-91	Dixon Gamble	1861-62	Richard Mann
1791-92	Dixon Gamble	1862-63	William Mann
1792-93	John Cooper	1863-64	John Mann
1793-94	John Cooper	1864-65	Charles Garneys
1794-95	John Cooper	1865-66	Frederick Barkway
1795-96	John Williams Plowman	1866-67	Henry Bellman

BUNGAY 1725-2007

Years	Name	Years	Name
1867-68	William Hartcup	1937-38	Rosalind Messenger
1868-69	Samuel Smith	1938-39	Leonard Buckell Cane
1869-70	Charles Childs	1939-40	Ronald Ernest Wightman
1870-71	Herbert James Hartcup	1940-41	Robert Rowland Hill Sprake
1871-72	Richard Mann	1941-42	Harry Nathan Rumsby
1872-73	Charles Garneys	1942-43	Reginald John Reynolds
1873-74	Frederick Barkway	1943-44	Reginald John Reynolds
1874-75	William Hartcup	1944-45	Ronald Ernest Wightman
1875-76	Henry Bellman	1945-46	Douglas Leslie Hewitt
1876-77	Samuel Smith	1946-47	Henry William Owles
1877-78	Herbert James Hartcup	1947-48	Cecil Baden Warnes
1878-79	Charles Garneys	1948-49	Cecil Cameron Rumsby
1879-80	Henry Bellman	1949-50	William Thomas Courtney
1880-81	William Hartcup	1950-51	Rosalind Messenger
1881-82	Samuel Smith	1951-52	John Marshall Clay
1882-83	Herbert James Hartcup	1952-53	Douglas Leslie Hewitt
1883-84	Edwin Haward & Henry Wightman	1953-54	Percy Jeans Sprake
1884-85	Henry Wightman	1954-55	Wilfred Henry Sutton
1885-86	Frederic Smith	1955-56	Hilda Nursey
1886-87	Edmund Palmer Norton	1956-57	Percy George Levick
1887-88	Henry William Owles	1957-58	Leonard Hugh Cane
1888-89	William David Walker	1958-59	Neville Mortimer Coe
1889-90	Robert Campbell Mann	1959-60	Vera Alice Stevens
1890-91	Henry Bellman	1960-61	Walter Hunt Wortley
1891-92	Herbert James Hartcup	1961-62	Jack Frederick Keightley
1892-93	Henry Wightman	1962-63	Cecil Harry Harris
1893-94	Frederic Smith	1963-64	Lilian Irene Trafford
1894-95	Frederic Smith	1964-65	Ronald Stanley Albert Duhy
1895-96	William David Walker	1965-66	Ronald Stanley Albert Duhy
1896-97	Robert Campbell Mann	1966-67	Reginald George McDaniel
1897-98	Herbert James Hartcup	1967-68	John Edward William Gibbs
1898-99	Henry Wightman	1968-69	Anthony Reginald Hood
1899-1900	Frederic Smith	1969-70	Herbert Frank Whyte
1900-01	William David Walker	1970-71	Herbert Frank Whyte
1901-02	Robert Campbell Mann	1971-72	John Charles Haylock Maidment
1902-03	Herbert James Hartcup	1972-73	Samuel Burton Nursey
1903-04	William David Walker	1973-74	Wyndham Mackray Jordan
1904-05	Robert Campbell Mann	1974-75	Ivor Gerald Baldwin
1905-06	Austin Cook Smith	1975-76	Lilian Irene Trafford
1906-07	Ernest Henry Wightman	1976-77	Michael Percy Belcher
1907-08	Henry Beaumont Owles	1977-78	Douglas Raymond Vernon Crockett
1908-09	Reginald Hope Walker	1978-79	Jack Frederick Keightley
1909-10	Herbert James Hartcup	1979-80	George William John Franklin
1910-11	William David Walker	1980-81	Mary Kent
1911-12	Ernest Henry Wightman	1981-82	Richard Walter Mighell Monks
1912-13	Charles Henry Geoffrey Ramsbottom	1982-83	David Colin Charles Richardson
1913-14	George Colborne	1983-84	Harald Rhys Gordon Pulford
1914-15	George Colborne	1984-85	John Richard Paul Woodcock
1915-16	John Oddie Kemp	1985-86	Cicely Mary Smith
1916-17	Gilbert Holland Ransome	1986-87	Rosemary Martin
1917-18	James Bedingfield	1987-88	John Victor Palin
1918-19	Alfred Webb Cocks	1988-89	Desmond Percy Scarle
1919-20	Frederick Robert Wightman	1989-90	Mary Kent
1920-21	William Richards Norman	1990-91	Graham John May
1921-22	Harry Nathan Rumsby	1991-92	Colin Roy Hancy
1922-23	Humphrey Jeans Sprake	1992-93	Diana Hamilton Belcher
1923-24	James Llewellyn Montfort Symns	1993-94	Peter Morrow
1924-25	Ronald Ernest Wightman	1994-95	James Herbert Jervis
1925-26	Charles Henry Lockitt	1995-96	Peter Duncan Scott
1926-27	Ernest Henry Wightman	1996-97	Terence George Reeve
1927-28	Samuel Fiske	1997-98	Betty Joan Warnes
1928-29	Alfred Webb Cocks	1998-99	Roma Hazel Went
1929-30	Horace James Inwards	1999-2000	Reginald George McDaniel
1930-31	Sidney John Owles	2000-01	Arthur William Fisher
1931-32	Herbert Ellis Rackham	2001-02	Susan Vera Curtis
1932-33	Leonard Buckell Cane	2002-03	Terence George Reeve
1933-34	Leonard Buckell Cane	2003-04	Diana Hamilton Belcher
1934-35	Charles Philip Parry-Crooke	2004-05	Stephen Glenn Went
1935-36	Hubert Earle Bowerbank	2005-06	Mary Kent
1936-37	Geoffrey Guy Sprake	2006-07	Maureen Davies

BIOGRAPHIES

It has seemed best to present each Town Reeve in a complete biography, which has meant taking certain liberties with chronology in the case of second and subsequent terms of office; however, the reader is referred to the foregoing lists for an accurate idea of the complete succession of Town Reeves over the period covered by this book. It is likely that any of the first eleven hereunder had served terms prior to 1725; however, none of these served again after the Feoffees appointed in 1753 began to assume office, and consequently the terms shown thereafter represent the total served by each incumbent.

1725-26
JAMES KING
He appears to have been the son of a similarly named father, and to have been close to the Nelson family, two of whom also served as Town Reeve.

1726-27, 1736-37, 1739-40, 1744-45, 1747-48, 1750-51, 1753-54
RICHARD NELSON
The son of 'old Dick Nelson', who was co-owner of Bungay Staithe and Navigation from 1704, Richard Nelson (Junior) Georgianised Rose Hall, Olland Street, and also owned much property in Bungay and the surrounding villages. He was a member of Bungay Gentlemen's Club, which is thought to have existed since the reign of Henry VIII: a charitable institution, it met monthly, at the King's Head or the Tuns, until its dissolution in 1782.

The Proclamation of the Accession to the Throne of George II was read at Bungay during the first of the above terms of office. Richard Nelson died, unmarried, on 24 October 1768, aged 68.

1727-28, 1740-41
JOHN KING
An apothecary and member of Bungay Gentlemen's Club, whose wife's name was Mary, he tried to promote Bungay as a spa, on the strength of an iron-containing spring in the grounds of the Castle. By 1728, the year in which he was first Town Reeve, he had completed a cold Bath House, which appears to have been a commercial success. In 1737 he published a book on hot and cold bathing, describing the rules to be observed by those of both sexes using his baths, and listing many case histories, concluding with that of a local man who, after a fortnight of treatment, recovered the use of his legs well enough to run away without paying for his immersions!

John King died on 5 June 1742, following a fall from his horse.

1728-29
JOSHUA NELSON

The cousin of Richard Nelson (seven times Town Reeve between 1726 and 1754), he was baptized in 1693, and became an attorney-at-law. He was a Churchwarden at St. Mary's, and died in 1738, survived for thirty-three years by his wife, Susanna.

1729-30, 1733-34, 1737-38, 1742-43
JOHN DALLING (Junior)

The son of John Dalling (Senior) (see next entry), he was an apothecary, and in 1729 married Catharine, daughter of Col. Windham of Earsham Hall; she died in 1738, aged only 28 - their son John, born c.1733, was appointed Governor of Jamaica in 1777 and became a Baronet in 1783. John Dalling was a member of the Gentlemen's Club from 1740 until his death, at the age of 47, on 4 July 1744.

1730-31
JOHN DALLING (Senior)

An apothecary, he in 1704 purchased Bungay Staithe and Navigation with Richard Nelson. He was also probably owner of the Manor of Bardolph. In March 1639 he purchased the ancient house in Earsham Street where horses' skulls were discovered in 1933. In 1707 he subscribed to the Articles of Belief of the Church of England, which were compulsory for certain professions. His wife, Susan, died, aged 44, in 1720. When he himself died, aged 68, on 17 April 1733, he left the Navigation and much property to his son, John Dalling (Junior) (see above).

1731-32
JOHN HEMBLEN

He is believed to have been the son of a father of the same name; his wife, Elizabeth, survived him by seventeen years when he died on 13 February 1756, aged 52.

1732-33
JOHN BOTWRIGHT

He may have been the father of Samuel Botwright (later Town Reeve), about whom more is known.

1734-35, 1738-39, 1743-44, 1748-49, 1751-52
THOMAS WALKER

He could have been the same Mr. Walker who, according to a reference in the St. Mary's Churchwardens' Book covering the year 1724 (no Christian name given) was Town Reeve for that year. Hannah Walker, wife of Thomas Walker, died in 1737.

1735-36, 1741-42, 1746-47, 1749-50, 1752-53
HENRY WILLIAMS

A woollen draper, and member of the Gentlemen's Club, he purchased in 1728 the Advowson of Ilketshall St. Andrew to provide an income for the Headmaster of Bungay Grammar School. He is believed to have lived in Duke's Bridge House, and he also owned land in Spexhall and Halesworth. He died in 1768, aged 79, followed five years later by his wife, Mary. He was a great benefactor of the Grammar School and is commemorated in a fine mural inside St. Mary's Church.

1745-46
ROBERT CLARKE

He was the second son of Gregory Clarke, who lived in Bridge Street House, where the French writer Chateaubriand, having fled from France, stayed during the winter of 1793-94. After his father's death in 1725 he inherited the house, and the extensive tanneries which he owned along the river banks. He was a member of the Gentlemen's Club, and died on 6 November 1748, aged 73, being buried inside St. Mary's Church.

1754-55, 1766-67
JOHN MEEN

The first Town Reeve from the twenty new Feoffees appointed in 1753, he worked at Bungay Staithe and was a member of the Gentlemen's Club. When Churchwarden at Holy Trinity, he sold a bell in order to enlarge the church. Mary Meen, possibly his wife, died on 6 November 1754, a month before he assumed the office of Town Reeve for the first time.

1755-56, 1767-68, 1775-76, 1782-83, 1789-90
JOHN VAN KAMP

He was an attorney-at-law and a member of the Gentlemen's Club, of which he became President in 1773. He lived in Earsham House, which he leased to Thomas Manning in 1798. He owned farms in Denton and Alburgh, and was a churchwarden at St. Mary's. His wife, Tabitha, was only 31 at her death in 1745; he had at least one son and two daughters, and died on 4 March 1800.

1756-57
EDWARD COOPER

A surgeon who practised for over thirty years in the town, he continued hydrotherapy on the Bath Hills after the death in 1742 of John King, whom he succeeded as Town Doctor. He rebuilt the Bath House in 1747, although it declined thereafter. For his care of the poor and control of infectious diseases he was paid by the Town Reeve £14 a year, and in 1750 he declared that Bungay was entirely free of smallpox. In 1753, he was registered by the Bishop to practise surgery.

Mr. Cooper was a member of the Gentlemen's Club, and died on 31 March 1764, aged 57. His commemorative marble mural in St. Mary's Church, of which he was a Churchwarden, carries an epitaph in Latin, paying tribute to the diligence, faithfulness and skill with which he practised the healing art.

1757-58, 1768-69, 1776-77, 1783-84, 1784-85
THOMAS MANNING

Born at Bridge Street House, Bungay, in 1724, he was the son of Thomas Manning of Starston and Bungay, who married Susan, sister of Robert Clarke (Town Reeve 1745-46). Thomas Manning (Junior) became a surgeon practising at Bungay, and was a Justice of the Peace for Suffolk. He lived in Earsham House, and was a member of the Gentlemen's Club and a Churchwarden at St. Mary's, and had an interest in archaeology, making a large collection of manuscripts relating to the town. He was also a Director of Shipmeadow House of Industry. He married Frances Simpson and their only child, Frances, born in 1749, married Thomas Jenkinson Woodward, LL.D., J.P. for Norfolk and Suffolk. When Mr. Manning died in 1787, aged 63, many of his Bungay records passed to his son-in-law.

1758-59
ROBERT WILLIAMS

He is thought to have been the son of Henry Williams (five times Town Reeve between 1735 and 1753). Robert Williams was a Churchwarden at St. Mary's and in 1762 surveyor of the highways of Bungay.

1759-60
WILLIAM LAMB

An eminent mercer and draper, he died on 28 November 1768, aged 59, followed in 1775 by his wife, Elizabeth. Their fine memorial mural is above the pulpit in Holy Trinity Church. During this term of office, George III succeeded to the Throne on the death of George II, and was proclaimed at Bungay on 3 November 1760.

1760-61, 1769-70
THOMAS PLOWMAN
   The son of a similarly named father, and his wife, Elizabeth, he was a leather currier, whose first wife, Mary, was aged only 32 at her death in 1734. He died in 1777, aged 82, followed in 1801 by his second wife, Elizabeth, at the age of 96.

1761-62
THOMAS PRENTICE
   He was a grocer, also owning property at Wrentham. He and his wife, Elizabeth, had at least two sons and a daughter. He died in 1782.

1762-63
ISAAC REEVE
   He may have been a schoolmaster. He converted the Cock Inn in Earsham Street to Bridge House, eventually selling it to John Scott (Senior). He was also a Churchwarden at St. Mary's. Following the death of his first wife, Sarah, he married secondly Anne, the widow of John Dell of Norwich; she also predeceased him. He died, aged 72, in 1771.

1763-64, 1770-71, 1777-78
WILLIAM PELL
   A Churchwarden at Holy Trinity and a member of Bungay Book Society, he lived at Duke's Bridge House, which he possibly built. He also owned property in Norwich. He had at least three daughters and is believed to have died in 1790.

1764-65, 1771-72, 1778-79
SAMUEL BOTWRIGHT
   The brother-in-law of Isaac Reeve (Town Reeve 1762-63), he was a saddler. He also owned public houses and two butcher's shops in Bungay, and farms in many local villages. He was a Churchwarden at St. Mary's and died in 1782, aged 84, predeceased by his wife, Katherine, in 1772.

1765-66, 1772-73, 1779-80, 1785-86, 1790-91, 1791-92, 1797-98
DIXON GAMBLE

A draper, he married Martha Borrett at Holy Trinity Church, Bungay, on 31 December 1758; one of their sons became a clergyman and another a soldier. In 1778 he placed weathercocks on St. Mary's Church, and in 1781 supplied material for the funeral of John Scott (Senior). At the end of his fifth term as Town Reeve he was reappointed to complete his improvements to St. Mary's churchyard. He died on 22 January 1800 and is buried at Thwaite with other members of his family.

1773-74, 1780-81, 1786-87, 1796-97, 1799-1800, 1801-02, 1803-04, 1805-06
NELSON BURTSAL

He was the nephew of Richard Nelson (seven times Town Reeve between 1726 and 1754), his father, William Burtsal, having married Mr. Nelson's sister, Frances. He lived in Rose Hall after his uncle's death, also owning the adjoining mill. An overseer of the parish of Bungay Trinity, he joined the Gentlemen's Club in 1768, resigning in 1782. He married Susanna Sparll at Holy Trinity Church on 26 February 1770; she outlived him by sixteen years after he died, aged 73, on 10 January 1808.

1774-75, 1787-88, 1792-93, 1793-94, 1794-95, 1798-99, 1800-01, 1802-03, 1804-05, 1806-07, 1807-08, 1808-09, 1809-10, 1810-11
JOHN COOPER (Senior)

The son of Edward Cooper (Town Reeve 1756-57), in 1803 he was one of the Commissioners of the Bungay Navigation. In 1809, being apparently the sole surviving Feoffee, it seems that he appointed forty-two others! He died, aged 72, on 16 July 1824, survived for twelve years by his wife, Mary.

1781-82, 1788-89, 1795-96
JOHN WILLIAMS PLOWMAN

The son of Thomas Plowman (twice Town Reeve), he was a tanner, operating from premises at Broome. He also owned houses and shops in Bridge Street, and a blacksmith's and wheelwright's shop at St. Cross South Elmham. He married Susanna Bellamy of Earsham in the church there on 21 October 1763; they had at least three sons and a daughter. A member of the Gentlemen's Club and of the Bungay Book Society, he died in 1799.

1811-12
MATTHIAS KERRISON

The third son of a yeoman farmer at Kirstead and Seething, he was born in 1742. He married Mary Barnes of Barsham on 22 May 1770, having a son and a daughter. In 1753 he became owner of Bungay Staithe and Navigation, where he amassed a fortune during the Napoleonic Wars by dealing in timber, coal and corn.

A merchant, tradesman, dealer and speculator, he became virtually a millionaire, buying vast estates in Suffolk and Norfolk. He also owned many public houses in Bungay, the beer and ale being supplied from his breweries in Bridge Street. He was a County Magistrate for Suffolk for over thirty years.

His wife, Mary, died in 1812, the year in which he was Town Reeve. Also during this year, he replaced the Corn Cross in Bungay Market Place with the new Town Pump - a plaque bearing a pastoral scene and the inscription "M.K. T.R. 1812" can still be seen on the site. His brother, Sir Roger Kerrison, twice became Mayor of Norwich.

Matthias Kerrison died on 12 April 1827, aged 85; a distinguished mural memorial to him and his wife may be found in Holy Trinity Church.

1812-13
WOLFRAN LEWIS

A surgeon and apothecary, he was a member of the Gentlemen's Club from 1755 to its demise in 1782. He lived in Earsham House, part of which he rented, it seems, for forty-seven years. He trained three apprentices from 1765 to 1770, and was a trustee of the Suffolk Benevolent Medical Society. In 1803 he was also a commissioner for Bungay Navigation, and in 1809 he treated John Barber Scott's mother when she was dying from scarlet-fever. His wife, Martha, died in 1812, just before he became Town Reeve; his son, John, became a clergyman at Thwaite.

He died on 26 April 1823, aged 93, and is buried in St. Mary's churchyard.

1813-14, 1814-15, 1815-16, 1816-17, 1817-18, 1832-33
JOHN SCOTT

He was born on 2 February 1756, and married Ann Sawyer, having one son. John Scott was a wealthy tradesman and businessman, described as a 'tanner, glover and fellmonger (dealer in skins)'. He was also engaged, in partnership with his brother, Samuel, in importing goods, mainly wool and timber, from Russia. They had tanneries along both sides of the Waveney near their houses - John Scott lived at Bridge House, Earsham Street, for sixty years of his life, and in 1811 he bought Waveney House, opposite, where his brother lived until his death in 1825. In 1814, at the onset of his five-year period as

Town Reeve, he lent the Feoffees £500 to pave each side of Earsham Street from his house to the Three Tuns on one side, and to the Swan on the other. The loan was free of interest and repayable at £100 per annum. In 1823, he lent the town a further £1,229 for street paving. He was generous to his family and to the poor. He died on 5 October 1836, aged 80.

1818-19, 1833-34
MATTHEW BRETTINGHAM KINGSBURY

Born on 31 May 1766, the son of William Kingsbury, maltster, and his wife, Elizabeth, who lived in Waveney House, he was an attorney in partnership with Mr. Margitson. He was a Churchwarden at St. Mary's and a member of the Bungay Book Society, and for many years kept an obituary list of prominent local people. He died on 25 February 1837, aged 71; his wife, Elizabeth, died in 1866.

1819-20, 1835-36
RICHARD MANN (Senior)

Born on 26 September 1777, he married Hannah Day, having several children, including three sons who were also to serve as Town Reeve. In 1813 he bought Bridge Street House, and in 1836 ordered the removal of the prisoners' cage from the Butter Cross. He was the Senior Churchwarden at St. Mary's, where his death on 6 March 1844, at the age of 66, is commemorated in a stained-glass window.

It fell to his lot early in 1820 to read the Proclamation of the Accession of King George IV, which event he commemorated at the end of the year by the presentation at the Town Meeting of a silver medal depicting the new King, to be worn by succeeding Town Reeves as an emblem of office. The inscription on the reverse reads:

'Presented to the Feoffees and Inhabitants of the Town of Bungay by Richard Mann, Town Reeve 1820, as a Token of his Esteem and to commemorate the Accession of George the Fourth to the Throne of Great Britain'.

1820-21, 1836-37, 1846-Sept. 1847
WILLIAM DENNY

Born c.1770, he was a farmer at Bungay, his wife's name being Charlotte. Queen Victoria was proclaimed at Bungay on her Accession to the Throne in June 1837, during his second term as Town Reeve. He died in office on 2 September 1847, owing the town funds a considerable sum of money! John Barber Scott took over for the remainder of the year of office.

FROM THE TOWN REEVES' BOOKS:

Almost all the Feoffees whose signatures appear below served at some stage as Town Reeve.

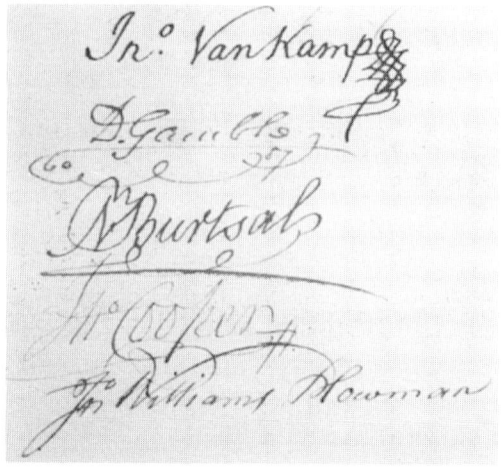

1795

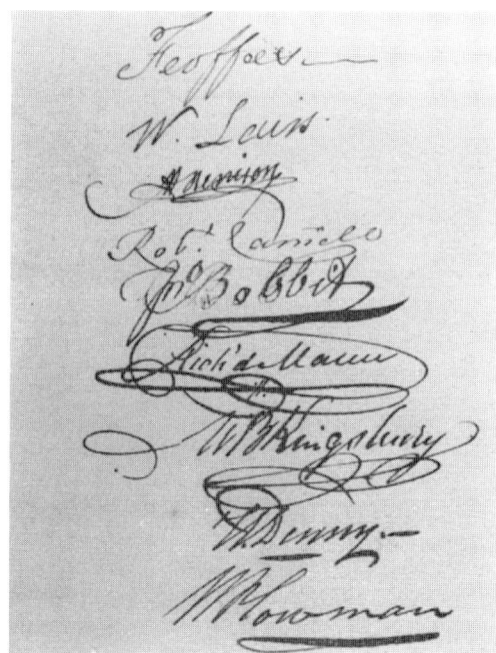

1818

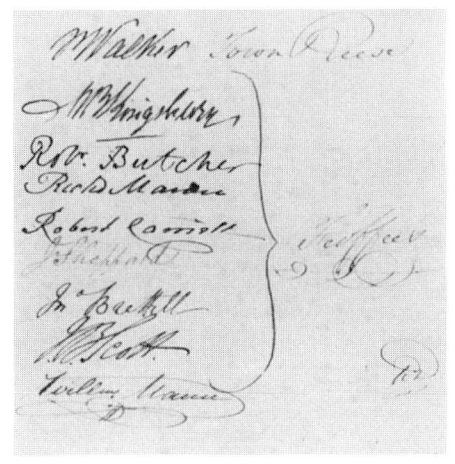

1830

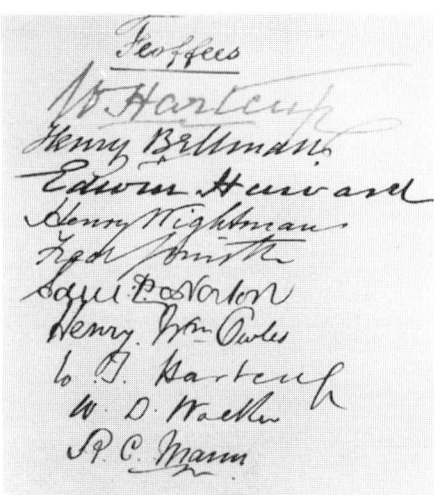

1883

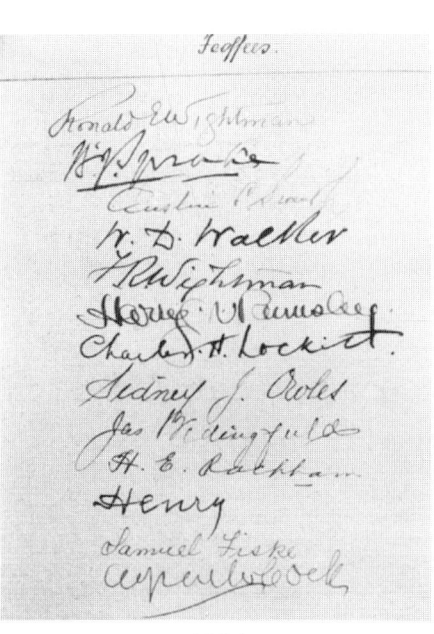

1864   1924

1821-22
MATTHIAS ABEL

This name was carried through at least four generations of the family, giving rise to some confusion; however, it is believed that this Matthias Abel was the son of Matthias Abel, draper, and his wife, Elizabeth, and that he became a grocer. In 1798 he was Treasurer of the Loyal Bungay Volunteers, and he died on 30 June 1827, aged 65. His son of the same name, sometime soldier and actor, who had been bankrupted following a most extravagant life, predeceased him in 1815 in London, and it appears to be his grandson, also Matthias Abel, who became a schoolmaster and Head Postmaster at Bungay.

1822-23, 1837-38
ROBERT BURTSAL (Senior)

The son of Nelson Burtsal (eight times Town Reeve), he was born c.1777, and married Lucy Long at Ditchingham Church on 3 May 1798, two of their sons also becoming Town Reeve. He was a corn miller, and died on 13 January 1841, aged 64.

1823-24
ROBERT CAMELL, M.D.

A surgeon in practice with Lancelot Davie, he lived in the Market Place at the corner of Broad Street with Bridge Street. Having lost his first wife, Sarah, in 1799, he married secondly Emily Vandeput, a widow of London, on 25 July 1801; following her death in 1827, he married a third time, this wife's name being Lois. He was a distinguished doctor who in 1806 attended a meeting to reform the medical profession. In 1814 he wrote a letter to the Ipswich Journal in favour of vaccination, and in 1822 supplied information to the famous surgeon, Astley Cooper, on a case of dislocation of the clavicle, treated by his partner.

When he was Town Reeve, he produced a plan for macadamizing the streets of the town, but it was not carried out until a later date. He retired to Ditchingham, and died on 5 July 1837, aged 77.

1824-25, 1838-39. 1839-40
JOHN BRETTELL

He worked as a surgeon at Bungay for over fifty years from 1793; his surgery was in Upper Olland Street, and in 1828 he was one of the three first surgeons appointed to the Bungay Dispensary. He was also a Private in the Loyal Bungay Volunteers and a member of the Bungay Book Society. He died, aged 75, on 5 February 1842, one year after his wife, Elizabeth.

1825-26
JAMES SHEPPARD

A gentleman of independent means, though possibly once a baker, he lived in Bridge Street. He was a Churchwarden at St. Mary's and a Private in the Loyal Bungay Volunteers. Following the death of his first wife, Rebecca, he married, on 27 April 1829, Caroline Poll. He died on 25 October 1841, aged 80.

1826-27
JOHN COOPER (Junior)

The son of John Cooper (Senior) (fourteen times Town Reeve!), he was commonly called 'the Adonis'. After nine years' education at Bungay, he went in 1797 to Gonville and Caius College, Cambridge. He was also a Cornet of the Blues, Captain of the East Norfolk Militia, and in 1798 First Lieutenant of the Loyal Bungay Volunteers. For a short time he was a clergyman. He moved to Cove Hall in April 1836, and died there on 22 March 1845, aged 65. His commemorative mural, with those of his grandfather and father, is inside St. Mary's Church.

1827-28
Lt.-Gen. Sir EDWARD KERRISON, Bt., K.C.B., G.C.H., M.P.

He was born at Staithe House, Bungay, on 31 July 1774, the only son of Matthias Kerrison (Town Reeve 1811-12). He ran away from home and enlisted as a common soldier, but through his gallantry he achieved some distinction, and a distinguished military career followed.

He served with the 7th Light Dragoons and the Hussars, and in 1815 was severely wounded at the Battle of Waterloo, where also his horse was shot under him. However, he continued with his regiment and was present at the surrender of Paris. He was nominated a Commander of the Bath, and was knighted on 5 June 1815; he was created a Baronet by his friend King George IV in July 1821. He married Mary Martha Ellice of Fife, having a son and three daughters. He inherited from his father the entire village of Breckles in Norfolk, the Maynard Estate at Hoxne, and the Cornwallis Estate at Brome and Oakley in Suffolk. He built the Oakley Park Mansion on the site of Hoxne Hall for himself.

Having represented the borough of Shaftesbury from 1812, and Northampton from 1818, he was first elected as Member of Parliament for Eye, Suffolk, in 1824, and re-elected at every subsequent election until 1852.

The only M.P. ever to have been Town Reeve of Bungay, he died in London on 9 March 1853, aged 78.

1828-29, 1841-42, Sept.-Dec. 1847, 1847-48, 1852-53, 1856-57
JOHN BARBER SCOTT

The only child of John Scott (six times Town Reeve), he was born on 24 February 1792 in Bridge House (now Scott House) in Earsham Street, Bungay. He was educated at Bungay Grammar School and Emmanuel College, Cambridge, where he further developed his ability in classics and mathematics. While still an undergraduate of 22 he met Napoleon on a visit to Elba in 1814, and in his diary recorded their conversation in French. While on other European tours he became fluent in German and Italian and when studying to enter the Church he learned Greek and Hebrew. He did not, however, become ordained as a clergyman, but after inheriting his father's fortune, devoted the rest of his life to philanthropy, chiefly in the field of education for the poorer classes. He never married.

From the age of seven he kept a diary which was discovered in an attic of Waveney House some sixty years after his death. Thanks to this record we know a great deal about the social life of the town and neighbourhood during the first half of the nineteenth century, and it is clear that the diarist himself was one of its most outstanding public figures. We are told that John Barber Scott was 'a man of striking appearance, fully six foot two in height, though he walked with a slight stoop. His hair was dark and he owned a pair of particularly piercing black eyes'. All his life a student and analytical observer of men and events, he died at Waveney House, opposite his birthplace, on 10 September 1862, aged 70.

1829-30, 1842-43, 1848-49, 1853-54, 1857-58
PEARSE WALKER

The son of Philip and Ann Walker, he was born at Attleborough, and baptized there on 29 May 1785. His wife's name was Georgia. A gentleman landowner, he was also a Churchwarden at St. Mary's and a member of Bungay Book Society.

The Accession of King William IV occurred during the first of his five terms as Town Reeve. He died, aged 74, on 18 September 1859 at his home on Flixton Road.

1830-31, 1844-45, 1850-51, 1855-56, 1859-60, 1862-63
WILLIAM MANN

He was born on 1 October 1806, a son of Richard Mann (Senior) (twice Town Reeve). With his brother, Richard Mann (Junior) (six times Town Reeve), he was a coal and corn merchant at Wainford Mill, Ditchingham; they erected maltings there in 1856. He never married, and died on 14 December 1878, aged 72.

1831-32
ROBERT AGGAS BURTSAL

The Nelsons and Burtsals, both prolific families, were closely related, and seven of them, with the same or similar names, served as Town Reeve. Some uncertainty arises, but this incumbent was probably the son of William Burtsal and Mary Aggas, who were married at Earsham in 1797. He may have been a wine merchant, and died on 15 February 1876, aged 70.

1834-35
ROBERT BUTCHER

He was baptized at Earsham on 5 March 1764, the son of Mark and Mary Butcher; for some time his family carried on the business of the Norfolk Distillery at Earsham. On 15 April 1789 at Earsham Church, he married Anna Maria Heyhoe. He became a wealthy landowner who from 1809 lived at 'The Grove', a mansion overlooking Bungay on the Flixton Road, which was later demolished and replaced by Upland Hall. There are many references to the Butcher family in J. B. Scott's diary, and it seems that Robert took some part in the public life of the town. He died from a stroke on 20 August 1844, aged 82.

1840-41
NELSON BURTSAL

Born c.1800, he was one of the sons of Robert Burtsal (Senior) (twice Town Reeve); his brother Robert was also to serve. He married Anne Currie at St. Mary's Church on 30 September 1841 while in office as Town Reeve.

1843-44, 1849-50, 1854-55, 1858-59, 1861-62, 1871-72
RICHARD MANN (Junior)

He was born in 1802, a son of Richard Mann (Senior) (twice Town Reeve). With his brother William (six times Town Reeve) he was a coal and corn merchant at Wainford Mill, Ditchingham. He died, aged 72, on 19 July 1875, having been predeceased by his wife, Maria.

1845-46, 1851-52
ROBERT BURTSAL (Junior)

He was baptized at Holy Trinity Church, Bungay, on 9 June 1803, one of the sons of Robert Burtsal (Senior) (twice Town Reeve), his brother, Nelson, also having served in 1840-41. He was a merchant at Ellingham, and also acquired 'The Grove' from the Butcher family. He died on 22 April 1856.

1860-61, 1863-64
Lt.-Col. JOHN MANN

Born in Bungay in 1805, a son of Richard Mann (Senior) (twice Town Reeve), he was for part of his life with H.M. East India Service, and later lived in retirement at Hedenham Hall. He was unmarried, and died on 8 July 1868, aged 62.

MATTHIAS KERRISON
Town Reeve
1811-12

Photograph by courtesy of
S. J. Govier / C. Piper
(Cleer Sewell Alger Photographic Collection)

JOHN SCOTT
Town Reeve
1813-14, 1814-15, 1815-16,
1816-17, 1817-18 & 1832-33

**Lt.-Gen. Sir EDWARD KERRISON,
Bt., K.C.B., G.C.H., M.P.**
Town Reeve
1827-28

JOHN BARBER SCOTT
Town Reeve
1828-29, 1841-42, Sept.-Dec. 1847,
1847-48, 1852-53 & 1856-57

WILLIAM HARTCUP
Town Reeve
1867-68, 1874-75 & 1880-81

CHARLES CHILDS
Town Reeve
1869-70
with his wife Emily

Col. HERBERT HARTCUP
Town Reeve
1870-71, 1877-78, 1882-83, 1891-92,
1897-98, 1902-03 & 1909-10

FREDERIC SMITH
Town Reeve
1885-86, 1893-94, 1894-95 &
1899-1900

1864-65, 1872-73, 1878-79
CHARLES GARNEYS, M.R.C.S., L.S.A.

Born at Kenton, Suffolk, he married Phoebe Robinson, having three sons and four daughters. He gained the qualifications of Member of the Royal College of Surgeons and Licentiate of the Society of Apothecaries at London University in 1816, and was for many years a surgeon practising in Bungay; he lived in Trinity Street House (now no. 19), which continued to be the home and surgery of succeeding doctors until 1977.

From 1827 until 1875 there are many references to Charles Garneys attending accidents and giving evidence at inquests. His three sons, Thomas, Henry and William, all became doctors, working with their father at Bungay at various times.

Charles Garneys, who was 88 when last Town Reeve, died on 31 December 1881, aged 90.

1865-66, 1873-74
Rev. FREDERICK BARKWAY

Born c.1801 at Hoxne, he was admitted a sizar at Emmanuel College, Cambridge, in 1823, but left after one year. He was ordained a Deacon at Norwich, and a Priest in 1825. He was Deputy Master of Bungay Grammar School from 1824 to 1858, occupying the school premises for some of that time. Having been Curate at Ilketshall St. Andrew, he later occupied the same position at Bungay. His wife's name was Mary Ann.

A great athlete, he was the only Town Reeve known to have been a clergyman, and died at Lavenham on 7 July 1875.

1866-67, 1875-76, 1879-80, 1890-91
HENRY BELLMAN

Born at Helmingham, Suffolk, he was a solicitor in Broad Street, Bungay, and for more than fifty years Clerk to the Magistrates. Following the death of his first wife, Elizabeth, he married secondly Laura Sevena Allsopp, who also predeceased him.

Mr. Bellman, who was remembered earlier last century as 'a man unbending in mind and body', exercised his autocratic right as Town Reeve by spending, against the will of his fellow Feoffees, a considerable sum of money from the town purse on repairs to the tower of St. Mary's Church, of which he was Churchwarden.

He died on 2 August 1896, aged 81.

1867-68, 1874-75, 1880-81
WILLIAM HARTCUP

Born at Ipswich on 23 March 1814, the son of a clergyman, he was articled to the Bungay legal firm of Kingsbury & Margitson in 1833, and was taken into partnership in 1839 by Mr. Margitson, succeeding to the entire business on the latter's death in 1848. On 13 June 1843 he married Mr. Margitson's eldest daughter, Louisa Jane, having five children; they lived at Upland Hall (formerly 'The Grove'), which he rebuilt. He was a Governor of the Grammar School and a Justice of the Peace for Suffolk. He raised £3,000 for the augmentation of the living of St. Mary's Church, of which he was for many years Churchwarden.

On the occasion of their Golden Wedding anniversary in 1893, Mr. and Mrs. Hartcup were presented by the inhabitants of Bungay with a beautiful silver candelabrum. This was given back to the town by the Hartcup family in 1958, since when it has been regularly used at the Town Dinner.

William Hartcup died on 24 September 1895, aged 81.

1868-69, 1876-77, 1881-82
SAMUEL SMITH

The son of Richard Smith, linen weaver, he was born at Bungay, his wife, Isabel, coming from Bramfield. He became a solicitor at Bungay, inheriting Earsham House, which his father had bought in 1830. He was chiefly noted for his generous sympathy with the poor and his good works. He died on 4 April 1888, aged 82.

1869-70
CHARLES CHILDS

Born in Luton in 1807, he took over the printing works run by his father, John Childs, on the latter's death in 1853; he married Emily Ray. The cultivation of music was one of his chief hobbies; he conducted a large singing class amongst his employees for many years, giving half-yearly concerts. He also in 1847 founded the choir of the Congregational Church, of which he was an ardent member, and became Captain of the Old 4th Suffolk Corps of the Volunteer Movement.

Five years after the famous episode of his father's imprisonment at Ipswich for non-payment of rates to the Church of England, Charles Childs was cited to appear for a similar refusal - however, he won his case.

He died suddenly at Bungay on 26 December 1876, aged 69.

1870-71, 1877-78, 1882-83, 1891-92, 1897-98, 1902-03, 1909-10
HERBERT JAMES HARTCUP

The eldest son of William Hartcup (three times Town Reeve), he was born at Ditchingham House on 13 October 1844, and educated at Rugby School. He joined the Volunteer Force in 1863, and was much later a Colonel, commanding the 2nd Voluntary Battalion of the Norfolk Regiment. He was admitted a solicitor in 1869, and six years later married Miss Fanny Selby-Lowndes of Rugby; they lived with their family at the Bank House in Broad Street. In 1900, Bungay Conservative Association was founded, with Col. Hartcup as Chairman. He was the Chairman of the Governors of Bungay Grammar School from 1880 until his death on 12 May 1914.

The last of his seven terms of office as Town Reeve saw the death of King Edward VII and the Accession to the Throne of George V, and in Bungay the formation of the Urban District Council.

1883-June 1884
EDWIN HAWARD

Born at Flixton, he was a master grocer and tea dealer in Earsham Street; his wife, Prudence, predeceased him. He died in office in June 1884, aged 64; Mr. Henry Wightman officiated for the remaining six months.

June-Dec. 1884, 1884-85, 1892-93, 1898-99
HENRY WIGHTMAN

Born on 24 August 1830 at Cransford, Suffolk, he married Mary Ann Hambling in 1857, having six sons and a daughter. In 1861 he founded the business of a draper and undertaker in Bungay Market Place, and was known throughout East Anglia as a trade valuer. Bungay's first County Councillor under the Local Government Act of 1888, he continued to serve until 1896.

For many years Chairman of the School Board and a Governor of Bungay Grammar School, he was Superintendent of the Sunday School at the Congregational Church, where he also served as Deacon for thirty-seven years, and was a founder member of the Bungay Nursing Institute.

He died on 18 September 1903, only a few hours after his fellow Feoffee since 1883, Mr. Frederic Smith.

1885-86, 1893-94, 1894-95, 1899-1900
FREDERIC SMITH

Born in 1833, the son of Samuel Smith (three times Town Reeve), his wife's name was Katherine. Admitted a solicitor in 1856, he practised first in conjunction with his father, and afterwards in partnership with his cousin, Austin Smith (later Town Reeve). A staunch Roman Catholic, he rebuilt St. Edmund's Church at Bungay as a memorial to his father. Later, the Roman Catholic School was rebuilt, also at his expense. In 1895, Mr. Smith built 'St. Edmund's Homes' in Outney Road, and presented them to the Town Trust.

He died on 18 September 1903, the same day as Mr. Henry Wightman, with whom he had been appointed a Feoffee in 1883.

1886-87
EDMUND PALMER NORTON

Born at Lowestoft on 17 October 1832, he was a solicitor at Bungay, and married Hester Worthington, a relative of the Scott family. His year of office saw the Golden Jubilee of Queen Victoria, and the foundation of the Bungay Nursing Institute. He died on 5 September 1893.

1887-88
HENRY WILLIAM OWLES

He was born in Bungay in 1838, the third son of Thomas Owles, wholesale grocer, who built the warehouse in Trinity Street. In 1863 he married Louisa Beaumont at Mendham, having a large family. He, also, became a wholesale grocer, and was Churchwarden at St. Mary's for twenty-one years. He died on 17 May 1893, aged 55.

1888-89, 1895-96, 1900-01, 1903-04, 1910-11
WILLIAM DAVID WALKER

He was born at Beccles in October 1847, and in 1873 married Sarah Elizabeth Hope of Manchester. In partnership with his brother, Arthur, he owned the navigation rights of the Waveney between Bungay and Beccles, where Matthias Kerrison (Town Reeve 1811-12) had made his fortune during the Napoleonic Wars. They operated a fleet of wherries of which the 'Albion' alone survives, and sails the Broads. These plied between Bungay Staithe, Beccles, Lowestoft and Yarmouth. The firm was responsible for the upkeep of the locks, and they owned Ellingham Flour Mill and the Staithe Maltings. In 1899 the old Elizabethan Staithe House was pulled down to make way for a large and expensive malt office.

Mr. Walker lived in Olland House (now 'Dunelm') in Lower Olland Street, and made a public footpath, known as 'The Folly', along Honeypot Meadow to the Congregational Church, where he was a Deacon for many years and Life Superintendent of the Sunday School. Following his wife's death, he married her sister, Mabel, having eight children in all, and became a Justice of the Peace for Suffolk in 1907.

Mr. Walker signalled his fourth term of office with the purchase of a fire escape for the town and neighbourhood, and at the Town Meeting in 1902 stated that 'Mayors and Lord Mayors were now quite common things, but a real live Town Reeve was as scarce as a Great Auk's egg!' His third term of office saw the death of Queen Victoria and the accession of King Edward VII. The Coronation of King George V took place during his fifth and final term.

W. D. Walker died on 6 August 1925.

1889-90, 1896-97, 1901-02, 1904-05
ROBERT CAMPBELL MANN

He was born on 21 April 1855, his father, Henry, an East India merchant, being another of the sons of Richard Mann (Senior) (twice Town Reeve). He carried on the business of maltings merchant, living at Wainford House, Ditchingham. He was a Justice of the Peace for Norfolk and Suffolk. He married on 18 August 1885 in Holy Trinity Church, Bungay, Hester Ethel Norton, daughter of Edmund Palmer Norton (Town Reeve 1886-87), and who later, as Ethel Mann, gained local fame as the author of 'Old Bungay'.

During his second term of office as Town Reeve, he presided over great festivities in Bungay in celebration of the Diamond Jubilee of Queen Victoria.

Mr. Mann had a stroke and died in church on 24 February 1924, aged 68; he and his wife are buried at Hedenham.

HENRY W. OWLES
Town Reeve
1887-88

W. D. WALKER
Town Reeve
1888-89, 1895-96, 1900-01
1903-04 & 1910-11

AUSTIN C. SMITH
Town Reeve
1905-06

ERNEST WIGHTMAN
Town Reeve
1906-07, 1911-12 & 1926-27

H. BEAUMONT OWLES
Town Reeve
1907-08

Dr. GEORGE COLBORNE
Town Reeve
1913-14 & 1914-15

JOHN O. KEMP
Town Reeve
1915-16

Dr. GILBERT RANSOME
Town Reeve
1916-17

1905-06
AUSTIN COOK SMITH

Born at Bungay on 5 April 1845, into a family of great benefactors of Roman Catholicism in the district, he was educated at Old Hall, Ware, Hertfordshire, and at Ampleforth, Yorkshire. In 1871 he married Susanna Crosby Brooks, and returned to Bungay, where he was for many years in legal practice with his cousin, Frederic Smith (four times Town Reeve).

Mr. Smith was the first of the 1903-appointed Feoffees to serve as Town Reeve; early in their year of office, he and his wife hosted a Town Reeve's Ball.

Mr. Smith, who later lived at Earsham, received mass on his 100th birthday, and died three years later, on 24 May 1948, at the age of 103.

1906-07, 1911-12, 1926-27
ERNEST HENRY WIGHTMAN

The eldest son of Henry Wightman (four times Town Reeve), he was born on 22 May 1860 at Saxmundham. The family moved to Bungay less than a year later when his father established the draper's business in the Market Place.

Ernest Wightman was educated at Bungay Grammar School and Framlingham College, and in 1887 married Miss Ellen Jane Farrow, having four sons and two daughters. He became a Feoffee in 1903, the year in which his father died and he took over the business. He became a Governor of Bungay Grammar School in 1904 and was a Manager of Bungay Council Schools from 1891 to 1934. He was a member of Bungay Bowls Club and of the Congregational Church, in which he held various offices, including that of Deacon. He became a Justice of the Peace for Suffolk in 1908, and was Chairman of the Bungay Bench. Also in 1908, he became Manager of Bungay Nursing Institute and Welfare Centre. Furthermore, he was a member and Vice-Chairman of Bungay Urban District Council from 1910 to 1917.

Mr. Wightman, who from his youth onwards wrote a diary of local events, is remembered in Bungay as a very outstanding public servant. He died on 2 June 1948.

1907-08
HENRY BEAUMONT OWLES

He was born in Bungay on 16 August 1865, the eldest son of Henry William Owles (Town Reeve 1887-88), and educated at Yarmouth Grammar School. He had intended to train as an architect, but owing to his father's early death he was obliged to carry on the family wholesale grocery business in Trinity Street. He also continued another family tradition by serving as Churchwarden of St. Mary's for twenty-three years. In 1891 he married Emma

Harriet Fyson at St. Philip's Church, Norwich; they had a son and a daughter, and the family lived in 'The Ollands' in St. John's Road, which was one of the oldest houses in Bungay, having escaped the fire of 1688.

Mr. Owles was a keen tennis player, and won a golf competition when he was Town Reeve. His year of office also saw the presentation of an historical pageant in the Castle grounds.

Mr. Owles died on 29 January 1926, aged 60.

1908-09
REGINALD HOPE WALKER

The eldest son of W. D. Walker (five times Town Reeve), he was born at Yarmouth on 13 August 1876, and educated at Leys School, Cambridge. He joined his father's firm, attending London Corn Exchange most Mondays. Married in 1910, he and his wife Kathleen had a son and two daughters. He was a Churchwarden at Holy Trinity Church, and was instrumental in promoting Bungay Races on the Common each Easter Monday. He was Air Raid Warden during the First World War.

On accepting office as Town Reeve, Mr. Walker advocated Bungay's seeking urban powers, and following public meetings in January 1909, these were obtained later in the year.

R. H. Walker died after a short illness on 6 June 1919, aged 42.

1912-13
CHARLES HENRY GEOFFREY RAMSBOTTOM, M.D., Ch.B.

Born in 1869, he began medical practice in Bungay in 1903, living in Waveney House, which had a surgery annexe at the back. He was a keen sportsman, his interests lying particularly with horses and pigeons.

During his year as Town Reeve six new Town Houses were built by the Feoffees with the consent of the Charity Commissioners.

Unfortunately, Dr. Ramsbottom had to leave Bungay in 1913 for health reasons, and was unable to complete his term of office; Mr. Ernest Wightman became Acting Town Reeve.

Dr. Ramsbottom died in Adelaide, Australia, in 1941.

1913-14, 1914-15
GEORGE COLBORNE, Ph.D., M.A., M.R.C.S., L.R.C.P., J.P.

He was born at Bungay on 6 June 1845 and educated at Bungay Grammar School, Western College, Plymouth, the Universities of London and Munich and the Middlesex Hospital. His first wife having died after only three years of marriage, he married secondly, in 1882, Miss Anne Louise Redgate.

Dr. Colborne, a Deacon of Bungay Congregational Church, was Medical Officer of Health to Bungay Urban District Council and to Wangford Rural District Council. He lived in 'Hillside', which he built in 1907.

The war having broken out during his first year as Town Reeve, Dr. Colborne was re-elected to serve a second term.

In relinquishing office after two years, Dr. Colborne presented a silver chain, which his wife had found, for the Town Reeve's medal of office, to replace the blue ribbon with which it had been worn for many years.

Dr. Colborne died at Havant, Hampshire, on 15 January 1929.

1915-16
JOHN ODDIE KEMP

Born on 6 November 1859 at the Bank House, Eye, he married Ida Agnes Gage in 1895, having three sons and a daughter. He came from Barclays Bank at Halesworth to be Manager of the Bungay branch of Barclay's Bank in 1900, and also served as Treasurer of the School Board. He wrote the narrative of the historical pageant held at the Castle in 1908. Mr. Kemp took a great interest in the town, and corresponded with a member of the Bigod family living in France. He died on 26 January 1954, aged 94.

1916-17
Dr. GILBERT HOLLAND RANSOME

He was born in 1873, a member of the Ipswich engineering firm. He was educated at Ipswich School and gained his medical qualification at St. George's Hospital. In 1900 he married Helen Louise Jones of Ongar, Essex, and went into practice at Bungay, living at 19, Trinity Street. He was the first man in Bungay to own a motor car, and before this period kept three horses in his stable. He served on Bungay Urban District Council for some years before becoming Town Reeve.

In 1921, ill-health obliged Dr. Ransome to retire from medical practice. Following some years at Walberswick, he moved to Scole, where, with improved health, he again became active in public service. Ransome Avenue, Scole, was named in honour of his contribution to public life.

He died in the hospital where he was once Medical Officer, All Hallows, Ditchingham, on 12 December 1962, aged 89. He left two daughters.

1917-18
JAMES BEDINGFIELD

Born in Bungay on 1 May 1862, the son of a steam sawyer and Methodist local preacher, he became a master butcher and smallholder. He married firstly in 1881, and following the death of his first wife, Louisa, he re-married

Florence May Plummer, a young widow, at Earsham in 1919, having a daughter and a son.

He became a Feoffee and Justice of the Peace, sitting at Bungay Courthouse. During the First World War he undertook varied duties, including the control of food distribution to the public and collecting funds for our Armed Forces. While Town Reeve, he became the only person ever to serve also as Chairman of Bungay Urban District Council, which post he held for the remaining thirteen years of his life. During this time he also served on the Suffolk County Council at Ipswich.

Mr. Bedingfield chaired the Means Test Committee during the recession and was a Governor of Bungay Grammar School when it moved from Earsham Street to its new premises in St. John's Road.

He died at his home, Verdun House in Wharton Street, on 15 November 1931, aged 69.

1918-19, 1928-29
ALFRED WEBB COCKS

Born in 1862 at Redenhall, the son of Jeremiah Cocks, he succeeded his father as a corn merchant in Bungay, and on 2 August 1893 married Julia Ellen Maddle, having one daughter. During his first term of office, many newly-cast street names were affixed, some bearing the inscription 'Peace Year, 1919: A. W. Cocks, Town Reeve'.

Mr. Cocks became Clerk to the Reeves of Outney Common and Stow Fen, and a Justice of the Peace. Ten years after his first term as Town Reeve, he undertook a further year of office, during which the Suffolk Agricultural Show visited Bungay.

He died in 1930.

1919-20
FREDERICK ROBERT WIGHTMAN

Born on 21 May 1865 at Bungay, he was the second son of Henry Wightman, and younger brother of Ernest Wightman, both former Town Reeves. For many years he carried on the business of gentlemen's outfitter at Norfolk House, St. Mary's Street. He was also Secretary of the Bungay Nursing Institute.

In 1895, he married Mary Ellen Sewell of Bridgnorth, Salop, having two daughters. He died on 15 May 1949.

1920-21
WILLIAM RICHARDS NORMAN

He was born in 1864 at Bungay, and on 31 October 1886 married Sarah Baker at St. Mary's Church, Bungay. In 1905 he took over the Three Tuns Hotel from his mother, later moving to the Fleece Hotel, from where three of his five daughters were married during his year of office.

A whitesmith, he became in 1895 Captain of the town's Fire Brigade, which he had first joined in 1877 as a strapboy, but he resigned shortly after his year as Town Reeve. He was also the town's official bill-sticker! He died in 1926.

JAMES BEDINGFIELD
Town Reeve
1917-18

ALFRED W. COCKS
Town Reeve
1918-19 & 1928-29

FREDERICK WIGHTMAN
Town Reeve
1919-20

WILLIAM NORMAN
Town Reeve
1920-21

HARRY N. RUMSBY
Town Reeve
1921-22 & 1941-42

HUMPHREY SPRAKE
Town Reeve
1922-23

Dr. JAMES SYMNS
Town Reeve
1923-24

RONALD WIGHTMAN
Town Reeve
1924-25, 1939-40 & 1944-45

1921-22, 1941-42
HARRY NATHAN RUMSBY

Born on 30 July 1868 at Staithe Road, Bungay, he took over in 1904 the extensive foundry and agricultural implement manufactory previously owned by the Cameron family. His long record of public service included twenty years as a member of Bungay Urban District Council, and at one time he represented the town on the East Suffolk County Council. He was an Oddfellow, and a member of the Congregational Church, where he was a Sunday School teacher for many years. He and his wife, Emily Rosa, had three sons.

Mr. Rumsby marked his first term of office as Town Reeve by the construction and donation of an iron footbridge over the River Waveney near 'Sandy'.

The interval of twenty years which elapsed before he again took office, during the war, is one of the longest known in the history of the Town Reeve.

Mr. Rumsby died in January 1945.

1922-23
HUMPHREY JEANS SPRAKE

Born in 1865 in the West Country, the son of a tailor, he came to Bungay as a clerk in the legal practice of William Hartcup (three times Town Reeve), which later became 'Sprake & Co.'. On 14 October 1885 he married Harriet Reeve.

Town Clerk since 1895, he was unanimously elected a life member of the Town Trust upon his resignation from the post in March 1922; later that year he became Town Reeve. For many years also Clerk to the local Magistrates, he played a major part in the formation in 1910 of the Bungay Urban District Council, which superceded the two Parish Councils of which he was Clerk.

During his year of office as Town Reeve, he raised a large sum of money for All Hallows Hospital, Ditchingham. He retired from his legal work in 1925 and moved to Kilmington in Devonshire, where he died in December 1945, aged 80.

1923-24
JAMES LLEWELLYN MONTFORT SYMNS,
M.A., M.D. (Cantab.), M.R.C.S. (Eng.), L.R.C.P. (Lond.)

Born in 1885, Dr. Symns joined Dr. Ransome (Town Reeve 1916-17) in partnership in 1911, but was absent in the R.A.M.C. during the First World War. He originally lived at 17, Trinity Street, next door to the surgery, but after his partner retired in 1921 he moved to Bridge House, the old home of the Scotts, where he extended the garden in order to provide a tennis court.

Dr. Symns was unable to chair the Town Meeting at the end of his year of office, Mr. Humphrey Sprake deputizing for him.

In 1929 he retired from general practice and obtained a Health Ministry post in Edinburgh. He maintained that the success of his application was in part due to his past appointment as Town Reeve of Bungay!

He retired to Bath, where he died in 1965, aged 80.

1924-25, 1939-40, 1944-45
RONALD ERNEST WIGHTMAN

Born on 11 October 1887, the eldest son of Ernest Wightman (three times Town Reeve), he was educated at Bungay Grammar School and Framlingham College, and later joined his father in the drapery business established by his grandfather. In 1914 he married Miss Catherine Hilda Brooks of Beccles, having two sons and two daughters. A member of Bungay Urban District Council from 1919, he became a Foundation Feoffee in 1922, and in the same year the Honorary Secretary of Bungay Lawn Tennis Tournament, which post he held until 1931. He was responsible for the organization of this annual event held on the Recreation Ground, acting also as referee. He later became President of the Norfolk Lawn Tennis Association. He continued his family's association with the Congregational Church, of which he became a Life Deacon, also serving at county and district levels; he was for twenty years Superintendent of the Sunday School at Bungay.

During his first year of office as Town Reeve, Mr. Wightman presided at the meeting at which Bungay Town Football Club was formed; he served it at different times as Chairman and Treasurer. Appointed for a second time early in the war, he also served as Captain of the Home Guard, and as Chief Billeting Officer for the 275 evacuees who arrived in Bungay in 1940. He was Chairman of both the National Savings Committee and the Food Control Committee. The last of his three terms of office saw VE Day.

At various times Mr. Wightman was Captain of the Golf Club, a member of Bungay Choral Society, Chairman of the Bench, a General Commissioner of Income Tax and President of Bungay Rotary Club.

Quite outstanding in every sphere of public activity, Ronald Wightman died on 13 August 1970, aged 82.

1925-26
CHARLES HENRY LOCKITT, M.A., B.Sc., F.R.Hist.S.

He was born in 1877 at Tulse Hill, and educated at Whitgift School and University College, London, where he gained his first degree in History in 1896, followed by those of B.Sc. in 1903 and M.A. in 1911. Following teaching posts at Rivington Grammar School, Lancashire, Horsham Grammar School, Sussex, and Solihull School, Warwickshire, he became Headmaster of Bungay Grammar School in 1911. He served as a Second Lieutenant in the Suffolk Volunteer Regiment from 1916 to 1918.

He was a member of Bungay Urban District Council from 1922 to 1928, and of the Council of the Incorporated Association of Headmasters from 1926 to 1930, and wrote books which were published. Following the death of his wife, Ann, he married secondly, in 1924, her sister, Helen.

Mr. Lockitt, who retired in 1937, travelled from his home in Sussex to a ceremony held when the Grammar School became comprehensive.

He died in Worthing on 14 September 1964.

1927-28
SAMUEL FISKE

Born in 1862, he was employed at the Caxton Press, Beccles, before coming to Bungay about 1909 to join the staff of the Reading Room at the Chaucer Press. He was one of the first officials of the Chaucer Institute, and was for very many years organist at Barsham Parish Church.

A widower at the time of his death, at the age of 87, in December 1949, he left two sons.

1929-30
HORACE JAMES INWARDS

Born in Luton in January 1880, he began his career at a very early age at a bakery in King's Lynn, working extremely long hours; he later worked in London. He served in the R.A.S.C., and was wounded in the Boer War. In 1903 he married Charlotte Bone Green, having four sons and a daughter.

In 1908 he came to Bungay to take over a small bakery and shop in St. Mary's Street; he also for six years from 1918 farmed 360 acres at Earsham, breeding Suffolk horses and large black pigs, with which he won many diplomas. He was a member of Bungay Choral Society and the Bowls Club.

On his last day as Town Reeve, Mr. Inwards opened the new Fire Station which had been built by the Town Trust, but was later handed over to the Urban District Council. He died on 29 May 1955.

1930-31
SIDNEY JOHN OWLES

Born at Bungay on 6 June 1872, he was the third son of Henry William Owles and brother of Henry Beaumont Owles, both former Town Reeves. Following his education at Bungay Grammar School, he became an auctioneer and land agent, first being articled at Yarmouth, and later forming the firm which became Read, Owles and Ashford. Having served in the South African war in 1900, he spent some years with the Norfolk Yeomanry. He married Nellie Violet Cross. A member of Bungay Urban District Council for two years from 1917, he was appointed a Feoffee in 1922.

A Churchwarden at St. Mary's and a life member of All Hallows, Ditchingham, Hospital Committee, he was also Secretary of Bungay Steeplechase Committee and a member of Henham Harriers. He worked in connection with the re-starting of Bungay Stock Market, and made the arrangements for the visit of the Suffolk Agricultural Show to Bungay in 1929.

He died in 1933, following a stroke which caused him to fall off one of his horses on Bungay Common. He was 60.

1931-32
HERBERT ELLIS RACKHAM

Born on 8 March 1875 at Lowestoft, he married Beatrice Nora Chapman, having a son and three daughters. He became Manager of Barclay's Bank at Bungay in 1918, following twenty-six years at the bank's Beccles and Great Yarmouth branches. Elected to Bungay Urban District Council in 1924, he served for two years as its Vice-Chairman. A Churchwarden at Holy Trinity Church and a Governor of Bungay Grammar School, he was also for many years President of the town's Bowling Club. He died on 7 March 1948, the day before his 73rd birthday.

1932-33, 1933-34, 1938-39
LEONARD BUCKELL CANE, M.D., B.Ch. (Cantab.), M.R.C.S. (Eng.), L.R.C.P. (Lond.), Lieut-Col., R.A.M.C.(T.), T.D.

Born in Peterborough on 22 May 1882, he was educated at Uppingham, King's College, Cambridge, and St. Bartholomew's Hospital, London. He returned to his home town, where he succeeded his father in medical practice, becoming Honorary Physician to Peterborough Infirmary in 1908. In 1912 he married Miss Margaret English, having two sons and two daughters. He saw active service throughout the whole of the First World War, including a period as ophthalmic surgeon in a military hospital in Cairo, and spells in India and Burma. He came to Bungay in 1921, to join Dr. J. L. M. Symns (Town Reeve 1923-24) in medical practice, and in 1929 became Chairman of the Suffolk Division of the British Medical Association.

Dr. Cane was undoubtedly the most outstanding Town Reeve in modern times, and was tireless in his efforts to enhance the importance of the ancient office, reviving several of its traditions which had lapsed. In particular he restored the Town Dinner which had not taken place for sixty years. He also temporarily restored the Wingfield Dinner and Sermon which, according to the will of Thomas Wingfield, dated 1593, had for centuries commemorated this founder and benefactor, and possibly first Master, of Bungay Grammar School in the reign of Queen Elizabeth I. Dr. Cane also began the custom of compiling scrapbooks of 'contemporary history' from newspaper cuttings; these have been maintained by each successive Town Reeve.

During Dr. Cane's first term of office, when the old Town Pump in the Market Place was replaced by a lamp standard, he arranged for it to be surmounted by the Black Dog weathervane, in commemoration of the famous legend of 1577, when such an animal, thought to be the Devil in disguise, ran wildly through St. Mary's Church during a violent thunderstorm, striking terror into those who had fled there for refuge.

CHARLES LOCKITT
Town Reeve
1925-26

SAMUEL FISKE
Town Reeve
1927-28

HORACE INWARDS
Town Reeve
1929-30

SIDNEY OWLES
Town Reeve
1930-31

H. E. RACKHAM
Town Reeve
1931-32

Dr. LEONARD CANE
Town Reeve
1932-33, 1933-34 & 1938-39

CHARLES PARRY-CROOKE
Town Reeve
1934-35

HUBERT BOWERBANK
Town Reeve
1935-36

Dr. Cane's major achievement, however, was the excavation of the badly neglected Bungay Castle, the work being financed from public appeals and undertaken by local unemployed under the supervision of an expert architect. In order to complete this project, he was asked to serve a second consecutive term as Town Reeve; he was later awarded an Honorary Fellowship of the Society of Antiquaries in recognition of this archaeological enterprise. Dr. Cane worked with Ethel Mann on her monumental history, 'Old Bungay', which was published during his second year of office.

Four years later, Dr. Cane became Town Reeve yet again. However, he was called away on active service at the outbreak of the Second World War in 1939, and Mrs. Rosalind Messenger deputized for the remainder of his third term of office.

When Dr. Cane retired from medical practice in 1954, he was presented by the Town Reeve and Feoffees with a silver salver, inscribed with the new Bungay coat-of-arms. He died at Playford, near Ipswich, on 28 January 1956.

1934-35
CHARLES PHILIP PARRY-CROOKE, J.P.

He was born on 13 August 1896 at Bournemouth. Commissioned in the 4th Battalion Suffolk Regiment, he was mentioned in dispatches while serving in France during the First World War. In the Second World War, in the newly-formed Pioneer Corps, he had command of African garrison troops in the Middle East and East Africa. He and his wife, Winifred Rosa, whom he married in 1921, had two sons; they lived at Rose Hall, Bungay.

Mr. Parry-Crooke became a Feoffee in 1933 and a member of the East Suffolk County Council the following year. He was also Chairman of Bungay Urban District Council, Chairman of the Governors of the Grammar School, President of the Bungay British Legion, President of the Bungay Branch of the League of Nations, a Churchwarden at St. Mary's for fifteen years, for many years Captain of the Golf Club, and for one year President of Bungay Town Football Club. He later became Chairman of the Blything Petty Sessions, Vice Chairman of the East Suffolk Quarter Sessions, Chairman of the East Suffolk Hospitals Board and Chairman of the East Suffolk County Council Education Committee.

In commemoration of the Silver Jubilee of King George V and Queen Mary, which took place during his year as Town Reeve, Mr. Parry-Crooke gave a further medallion and an additional chain to be incorporated into the insignia of office. He was responsible for the local celebrations and commemorative events, and was awarded the King's Silver Jubilee Medal. He was also the donor of the banner of the Bigod family which flew from Bungay Castle for the first time on Jubilee Day.

On moving to Friston, near Saxmundham, in 1948, Major Parry-Crooke resigned from the Town Trust, but he and his wife always maintained close links with Bungay. He died on 28 November 1978.

1935-36
HUBERT EARLE BOWERBANK, D.C.M.

Born on 8 October 1881 at Norton, Stockton, Co. Durham, he came to Bungay in 1908 to take up an appointment at the Chaucer Press, becoming Assistant Manager in 1914; many years later he became a Director and Works Manager.

Mr. Bowerbank, who married a Bungay girl, Miss Polly Robertson, in 1911, having a son and three daughters, was a founder member of Bungay Amateur Dramatic Society, acting as Producer and Stage Manager. He became a Foundation Feoffee in 1933. Having been Captain of Bungay and Waveney Valley Golf Club for three years from 1927, he was its Vice-President at the time of his nomination as Town Reeve.

In January 1936, on the death of King George V, Mr. Bowerbank, at a ceremony in Bungay Market Place, read the Proclamation of King Edward VIII's Accession to the Throne. To mark this event, and his year of office, he created the children's playground on the Common, fencing off an area by the river, and equipping it with swings, see-saw and climbing frame.

He died in a London hospital on 19 December 1946.

1936-37
GEOFFREY GUY SPRAKE, M.A., LL.B.

Guy Sprake was born at Bungay on 5 November 1898, the third son of Humphrey Jeans Sprake (Town Reeve 1922-23), and educated at Bungay Grammar School and Downing College, Cambridge, although his law studies were interrupted by the First World War, which took him to Macedonia and Turkey. Returning to Bungay, he joined the legal firm of Sprake & Co. founded by his father. A keen sportsman, he rowed for his college, and was associated with Bungay and District Rifle Club. For many years he was Clerk to the East Norfolk River Catchment Board. He also took part in amateur dramatic productions. He lived with his wife, Doris, and their family at Earsham.

Only a few days after his nomination as Town Reeve, Mr. Sprake was called upon to read, at a ceremony in Bungay Market Place, the Proclamation of the Accession of King George VI, following the Abdication of his brother, Edward VIII. In commemoration of the Coronation which took place later in his year of office, Mr. Sprake raised money to provide a children's playground on the Jubilee Road housing estate. He also added a further commemorative medallion to the chain of office.

At his death on 15 August 1983, he had just completed sixty years as a member of the Law Society.

1937-38, 1950-51
Mrs. ROSALIND MESSENGER, M.B.E., J.P.

Miss Rosalind Haslett was born at Worth, Sussex, on 4 February 1902. Following a business training in London, she came to Bungay in 1926 as the first Secretary of the newly-formed Bungay Gas and Electricity Company Ltd., and in 1930 she married Mr. Ernest Messenger, the firm's Engineer and Manager. In 1931 Mrs. Messenger was appointed a Director of the company. In 1935 she was elected to the Bungay Urban District Council, and the following year became the first woman member of the Town Trust.

Shortly after her historic nomination in 1937 as the first woman Town Reeve of Bungay, and one of the youngest ever, Mrs. Messenger broadcast to America on the office, her script being prepared by Dr. Leonard Cane. She acquired the Castle Hills, scheduled under the Ancient Monuments Acts, for the Town Trust, and at a gala fête held in the grounds in the summer of 1938, the site was opened by Lady Stradbroke, who unlocked the iron gates, newly-wrought in Bungay and featuring the arms of the Earls of Bigod. Mrs. Messenger commemorated her year of office by adding to the Town Reeve's chain of office a medallion depicting Bungay Butter Cross.

Mrs. Messenger was the Honorary Secretary of the Bungay Nursing Institute, a post she was to hold for over forty years. She was the first woman Chairman of the Urban District Council from 1941 to 1945, and Chairman of the Invasion Committee during the war. She was also W.R.V.S. organizer for seven years from 1939. For over thirty years she was a representative member of the Education and other committees of the East Suffolk County Council, and a Governor of the Modern and Grammar Schools at Bungay from 1939 to 1974. Mrs. Messenger was associated with the work of the St. John Ambulance Brigade for Suffolk, at local and county levels, from 1946, and County Superintendent (N) in 1958. She was invested as an Officer of the Order that year. A Justice of the Peace from 1941, she was also a General Commissioner of Income Tax for the Wangford Division, and Chairman for several years.

Mrs. Messenger's husband died in 1949. For her work as Chairman of the Lowestoft and Waveney Youth Employment Committee, she was awarded the M.B.E. in 1950, and later the same year became Town Reeve again. During this second term, the Festival of Britain was celebrated in Bungay with a week of festivities, the main event being a pageant on the Castle Hills featuring the history of the town. Some 1,300 people were present at the last performance. Her distinguished sister, Dame Caroline Haslett, whose biography, 'The Doors of Opportunity', Mrs. Messenger later wrote, was principal guest at the Town Dinners at the end of both of her terms as Town Reeve. On relinquishing office for the second time, Mrs. Messenger presented a chain and medallion, being a replica of that commemorating her first term, to be worn by the Consort of the Town Reeve on special occasions in succeeding years.

Mrs. Messenger travelled widely from the 1930's, attending many international congresses, including the 4th United Nations Congress on the Prevention of Crime and Treatment of Offenders, held in Japan in 1970, and visited prisons in many parts of the world. She was a member of the Board of Visitors of H.M. Prison, Blundeston, for twelve years, for the last six of which she was its Chairman. A keen gardener throughout her life, she was a Vice-President of Bungay Horticultural Society.

In 1986, Mrs. Messenger celebrated her 50th anniversary as a member of the Town Trust with her fellow Feoffees, and the naming of 'Messenger Close', Bungay, will serve as a permanent tribute to her remarkable achievements and outstanding record of service to the town.

Mrs. Messenger died on 27 September 1990.

1940-41
ROBERT ROWLAND HILL SPRAKE

The youngest son of Humphrey Jeans Sprake (Town Reeve 1922-23), he was born at Bungay on 2 December 1900 and educated at the Grammar School. He proceeded in 1917 to Glasgow University to study science and surveying, and three years later to St. John's College, Cambridge, where he specialized in agriculture. Following some years at Diss, he returned to Bungay as an auctioneer, valuer and surveyor. He was at various times a member of Bungay Urban District Council and Depwade Rural District Council, Vice-Chairman of Earsham Parish Council, Air-Raid Warden for Earsham, Secretary of Bungay Race Committee and Clerk to the Outney Common and Stow Fen owners.

During Mr. Sprake's year of office as Town Reeve, the famous statue of Justice, having been removed for reasons of safety during the war from the Butter Cross, where it was first placed in 1753, was buried in the garden of his home at Earsham, where he lived with his wife, Rita.

Mr. Sprake died in 1972.

1942-43, 1943-44
REGINALD JOHN REYNOLDS

He was born at Mettingham on 15 July 1899 and educated at Wingfield Street Council Schools, Bungay. Following his apprenticeship to the Bungay branch of the International Stores, he became local Manager, and also spent four years at other of the firm's shops in the south of England. Returning to Bungay in December 1928, he started in business on his own account, eventually acquiring grocery shops in the Market Place and at Flixton Road, where he was Sub-Postmaster for eight years from 1937.

GUY SPRAKE
Town Reeve
1936-37

Mrs. ROSALIND MESSENGER
Town Reeve
1937-38 & 1950-51

ROBERT SPRAKE
Town Reeve
1940-41

REGINALD REYNOLDS
Town Reeve
1942-43 & 1943-44

DOUGLAS HEWITT
Town Reeve
1945-46 & 1952-53

HARRY OWLES
Town Reeve
1946-47

CECIL WARNES
Town Reeve
1947-48

CECIL RUMSBY
Town Reeve
1948-49

Elected to Bungay Urban District Council in April 1935, he shortly afterwards became one of its representatives on the Town Trust. He joined the Civil Defence organization in 1937, and early in 1942 became a part-time member of the National Fire Service. He also served on the committee of Bungay Town Football Club.

As a war-time Town Reeve he was very active in the interests of National Savings, and organized a huge collection of books for salvage.

At the Town Meeting in December 1943, Mr. Reynolds was re-appointed to serve a second consecutive term. After his double term of office, he was appointed as a Magistrate to the Bungay Bench, and many years later served as Secretary to the Bungay and Waveney Valley Golf Club. He and his wife, Winifred, had two daughters; he died on 19 March 1971.

1945-46, 1952-53
DOUGLAS LESLIE HEWITT, M.A., J.P.

Born on 26 January 1902 at Kirby Malzeard, Ripon, and educated at St. John's School, Leatherhead, Surrey, and Selwyn College, Cambridge, where he graduated in classics, he began his teaching career at his old school, and following posts at Wyggeston Grammar School, Leicester, and King Edward's School, Birmingham, he was appointed to succeed Mr. C. H. Lockitt (Town Reeve 1925-26) as Headmaster of Bungay Grammar School in 1937.

During the war years, he served as Deputy Chief Warden for Bungay, and was also co-opted onto the Urban District Council. He was appointed a Foundation Feoffee in 1945, becoming Town Reeve later the same year. During this term of office he presided over the Peace celebrations in Bungay, which included dancing in Broad Street until midnight.

Mr. Hewitt was Chairman of Bungay Urban District Council for two years from 1948, and became a Justice of the Peace in 1949. He served as Vicar's Warden at Holy Trinity Church, Chairman of Bungay Choral Society, President of the Bungay Division of the St. John Ambulance Brigade, and Chairman of Bungay Nursing Institute. For many years he was responsible for secretly composing humorous verses to be added to the song 'Old Bungay', sung at the annual Town Dinner.

During his second term of office as Town Reeve Mr. Hewitt presided over the celebrations in Bungay of the Coronation of Queen Elizabeth II. He retired from the Grammar School in 1961, and resigned from the Town Trust in 1977. He lived with his second wife at Geldeston. By his first wife, Josephine Bell Rose, he had three sons.

Mr. Hewitt died on 28 August 1994.

1946-47
HENRY WILLIAM OWLES

Harry Owles was born at Bungay on 20 August 1911 and educated at the Falconberg School at Beccles and at Bungay Grammar School. He practised as an auctioneer from 1928, becoming a partner in the firm of Read, Owles & Ashford on the decease in 1933 of his uncle, Sidney Owles (Town Reeve 1930-31). During his war service with the Royal Artillery he was taken prisoner in Greece, was moved to Germany, and following a period in hospital was repatriated in 1944. In 1955, he became Manager of the East Anglian Trustee Savings Bank at Beccles, and some five years later took over the same position at the Bungay branch. However, he was obliged to retire prematurely on account of ill health.

Mr. Owles, who served one three-year term on Bungay Urban District Council, was also Treasurer of the town's Conservative Association, and a keen member of the Bungay and District branch of the British Legion, whose annual Whitsun fête was held in the grounds of his home, 'Trees'. He and his wife, Freda, had a son and a daughter.

Harry Owles was the fourth member of his family to serve as Town Reeve, assuming office at a very early age. During his year of office the famous statue of Justice was retrieved from its place of safety (see 1941) and restored to its position on top of the Butter Cross.

Mr. Owles died on 29 November 1969, aged 58.

1947-48
CECIL BADEN WARNES

He was born at Bungay on 27 March 1900, and following his education at Bungay Grammar School joined the corn and seed business in the Market Place started by his father. In the First World War he served with the Bedfordshire Regiment, and during and after the Second World War was in the Special Constabulary at Bungay.

Created a Foundation Feoffee in 1945, he became a founder member and the first president of Bungay Rotary Club in the same year as assuming the office of Town Reeve.

A lifelong member of Holy Trinity Church, which he served as Churchwarden, Mr. Warnes was founder President of Bungay Players and a member of the Choral Society. Early in his year of office as Town Reeve, he was elected first President of the newly-formed Bungay Chamber of Trade. The Town Dinner at the conclusion of this year was the first to be held for ten years, the event having been suspended during the war.

Mr. Warnes died on 28 March 1985, the day after his 85th birthday, followed only five days later by his wife, Florence. They had a son and a daughter.

1948-49
CECIL CAMERON RUMSBY

The son of Harry Nathan Rumsby (twice Town Reeve), he was born at Earsham Street, Bungay, on 7 February 1905 and educated at Bungay Grammar School. He obtained an engineering degree at Northampton College, London University, and returned to join his father in the family firm of agricultural engineers, taking over with his brother after their father's death in January 1945. Co-opted onto Bungay Urban District Council during the war, he served for four years, and was appointed to the Town Trust in 1945 as a Foundation Feoffee.

During the war Mr. Rumsby was a Special Constable, and served in the Home Guard. He was at various times a Scoutmaster, President of the Bungay Grammar School Old Boys' Association, a Governor of the County Modern School, Chairman of the Chaucer Institute, and a magistrate. He had a keen interest in football and cricket.

During his year of office as Town Reeve, he attended the opening of the new Sports Field at the Maltings Meadow, Ditchingham, and crowned 'Miss Bungay' at the Battle of Britain and Shopping Week.

Mr. Rumsby and his wife, Ada, had two sons and a daughter. He died on 17 August 1966, aged 61.

1949-50
WILLIAM THOMAS COURTNEY

Born on 3 December 1903 at Leytonstone, he lived in London until 1937, when he moved with his wife, Rose, to Bungay to become Manager of the Book-Binding Department at the Chaucer Press; he had previously been Production Manager of a firm in Esher, Surrey.

The founder Secretary of Bungay Rotary Club, he was also Chairman of the town's Chamber of Trade, and was elected to the Urban District Council in 1947.

During his year of office, the Wings for Victory celebrations in the town were opened by the comedienne, Beryl Reid.

Mr. Courtney died on 28 April 1968, the day after his Ruby Wedding Anniversary.

1951-52
JOHN MARSHALL CLAY

He was born on 12 June 1919 at Highgate, London. Educated at Marlborough College, he left there in 1936 to go through the printing works of J. M. Dent & Sons at Letchworth. He joined the family firm of Richard Clay

& Co. in the autumn of 1937 in London, and was sent to Bungay at the beginning of the following year. He joined the Norfolk Yeomanry T.A. and was called up at the outbreak of war in September 1939. He was evacuated from Dunkirk, and after being commissioned in January 1941, was sent to India fourteen months later. He was wounded in Burma in June 1945 and demobilized the following year with the rank of Captain. He returned to the Company in October 1946, becoming Joint Managing Director in 1961 and Chairman in 1976, retiring in 1981. In 1948 he married Helen Margaret, daughter of Dr. L. B. Cane (thrice Town Reeve). They had a son and two daughters, one of whom was born during Mr. Clay's year of office.

Mr. Clay was Secretary of the Chaucer Institute for about thirty years and served at various times as President of the Bungay British Legion and of the town's Football and Cricket Clubs. He was a Governor of the old Grammar School and of the new High School for over twenty years.

In 1951 John Clay became the youngest Town Reeve in modern times at the age of 32. On 8 February 1952, he was called upon to read the Proclamation of the Accession of Queen Elizabeth II at a ceremony in Bungay Market Place. He donated a specially designed maroon gown to the Town Trust for the use of all future Town Reeves, to be worn on ceremonial occasions. This is now on display in Bungay Museum (see p. 93).

Mr. Clay died on 4 October 1999.

1953-54
PERCY JEANS SPRAKE

The eldest son of Humphrey Jeans Sprake, and brother of Guy and Robert Sprake, all of whom served as Town Reeve, he was born in Bungay on 8 September 1886. He founded the firm of Sprake & Co., which practised in succession to Hartcup & Son. During the First World War, he served with the Royal Artillery. He purchased Waveney House from Dr. Ramsbottom (Town Reeve 1912-13), living there for the rest of his long life. He and his wife, Brenda, had three sons and two daughters.

Upon the formation of Bungay Urban District Council in 1910, he was appointed its first Clerk, retaining this post for forty years, and in March 1922 succeeded his father as Clerk to the Town Trust; he was appointed a Foundation Feoffee in 1951. He was also Clerk to Bungay Magistrates for twenty-six years until 1952, and Churchwarden at St. Mary's for thirty-four years. A keen angler, he presented many trophies to Bungay Cherry Tree Angling Club.

The first person to have been Town Reeve and Town Clerk at the same time, his advice was often sought on the history and traditions of the Town Trust, on which he was regarded as a leading authority.

Mr. Sprake marked his year of office as Town Reeve by adding to the chain of office a medallion depicting Bungay's newly-granted coat-of-arms. He was within two months of his sixtieth anniversary as Clerk to the Town Trust when he died, on 23 January 1982, aged 95.

W. T. COURTNEY
Town Reeve
1949-50

JOHN CLAY
Town Reeve
1951-52

PERCY SPRAKE
Town Reeve
1953-54

WILFRED SUTTON
Town Reeve
1954-55

Mrs. HILDA NURSEY
Town Reeve
1955-56

Dr. PERCY LEVICK
Town Reeve
1956-57

Dr. HUGH CANE
Town Reeve
1957-58

NEVILLE COE
Town Reeve
1958-59
with Mrs. Margaret Coe
at the Town Dinner, 1959

1954-55
WILFRED HENRY SUTTON

Born on 28 December 1895 at Loddon, the son of a farmer and butcher, he started work as an engineer, but established with his brother a butchery business at Acle; he and his wife, Lily, were married there. In 1931 he bought a pork butcher's shop in St. Mary's Street, Bungay, and another similar business eight years later in the same street.

Co-opted onto Bungay Urban District Council during the war, he served as its Chairman from 1952 to 1954. He became a Feoffee in 1951. A lifelong Methodist, he was Steward of the local circuit and for very many years a local preacher. A keen Norwich City supporter, he was Chairman of Bungay Town Football Club for seven years from 1955, and was a founder member of Bungay Rotary Club.

During his year of office as Town Reeve, Mr. Sutton welcomed to Bungay the Countess Edwina Mountbatten of Burma at the inspection she carried out as Superintendent-in-Chief of the St. John Ambulance Brigade. He presented to the Town Trust a specially designed Tudor-style hat for the Town Reeve to wear on ceremonial occasions.

Mr. Sutton died on 19 November 1981.

1955-56
Mrs. HILDA NURSEY

Miss Hilda Burton was born on 7 September 1890 at Tibenham, and in 1915 married Mr. Samuel Parker Nursey; they had a son and a daughter. After her husband's death in 1932, Mrs. Nursey decided to carry on the family concern of leather merchants and glove manufacturers, the oldest business in Bungay, having been established in 1790.

First nominated to the Town Trust by Bungay Urban District Council, to which she was elected in 1938, she became a Foundation Feoffee in 1951. As Women's Royal Voluntary Service Centre Organizer after the war, she did outstanding work in helping sufferers of the East Coast Flood Disaster of 1953; she was also Chairman of the Ambulance Appeal Committee of the Friends of St. John, and for four years directly after the war she was Chairman of the Housing and Health Committee of the U.D.C. She was active in welfare work with the Civil Defence Corps, was a founder member of Bungay and District Chamber of Trade, and also a Governor of Bungay Grammar School.

As only the second woman to become Town Reeve, Mrs. Nursey accepted an honour which her late husband had twice had to decline for health reasons. She was awarded the British Empire Medal in 1968 for her services with the W.R.V.S., and died on 24 May 1977.

1956-57
PERCY GEORGE LEVICK,
B.A., B.Chir. (Cantab.), M.R.C.S., L.R.C.P. (Eng.)

Born on 16 October 1901 at Havant, Hampshire, he was educated at Epsom College, Pembroke College, Cambridge and St. Bartholmew's Hospital, London. He came to Bungay in 1930 to join Dr. J. H. Busteed in medical practice, continuing on his own account after the latter's retirement in 1937.

For some years Medical Officer of Health for Bungay Urban District and Wangford Rural District, he was much involved in the work of All Hallows Hospital, Ditchingham, and was also the town's Blood Transfusion Officer. He served on Bungay Urban District Council for one three-year term. A Governor of Bungay Grammar School, he was also Secretary, and later Captain, of Bungay and Waveney Valley Golf Club. He also took part in amateur dramatics.

On handing over the office of Town Reeve to his successor, he presented to the Town Trust a specially designed pennant to be flown from the Town Reeve's car.

Dr. Levick retired in 1976. Twice a widower, he had one daughter. He died on 7 January 1987.

1957-58
LEONARD HUGH CANE,
M.A., M.B., B.Chir. (Cantab.), M.R.C.S., L.R.C.P. (Eng.)

Born on 21 May 1913 in Peterborough, he moved to Bungay in 1921 when his father, Dr. Leonard Cane (three times Town Reeve), took up medical practice in the town. Hugh Cane was educated at Gresham's School, Holt, King's College, Cambridge, and St. Bartholmew's Hospital, London.

Following ten years with the Colonial Medical Service in Tanganyika, East Africa, he returned to Bungay, joining his father in practice in 1951, and taking over when the latter retired three years later. He served on the Bungay Urban District Council for thirteen years, and was elected Chairman of the successor Town Council in 1976. He was appointed a Foundation Feoffee in 1951 and, carrying on his father's keen interest in the preservation of Old Bungay, he undertook during his term of office as Town Reeve considerable improvements to the Castle grounds, and continued, as Custodian, to care for the ruins. In 1962 he founded the Bungay Museum, of which he was Curator. He also classified some two hundred Town Trust documents dating from 1561, and transferred them to the Suffolk Record Office. In 1985 he compiled an up-to-date set of maps of the Town Lands and had them bound in leather as a successor to the magnificent volume of 1857.

Dr. Cane and his wife, Margaret, had two sons and a daughter. He died on 29 March 2000.

1958-59
NEVILLE MORTIMER COE

Born on 16 February 1903 at Cavendish and educated at Woodbridge, he began a career with Barclay's Bank in 1921, coming to the Bungay branch in 1931 as cashier. Having been further transferred to Lowestoft, he returned to Bungay as Manager in 1955.

Elected to Bungay Urban District Council in 1956, he became a Councillor Feoffee, later being appointed a Foundation Feoffee. He served Bungay and District Chamber of Trade as Secretary and President, and was Chairman of the town's National Savings Committee and Treasurer of the Rotary Club. For some years Secretary of the Bungay and District Horticultural Society, he later became a Vice-President. A keen gardener, he entered many exhibits, particularly chrysanthemums, at the annual shows, and won numerous prizes. His wife, Margaret, was a physiotherapist; by his first wife he had a son.

During his year as Town Reeve, Mr. Coe raised over £1,000 for central heating at All Hallows Hospital, Ditchingham.

Mr. Coe died on 17 February 1988, the day after his 85th birthday.

1959-60
Mrs. VERA ALICE STEVENS

Miss Vera Dunnett was born on 17 January 1908 at Grundisburgh, and married there in 1933, having been a teacher for some years following her training at Norwich Training College. She came to Bungay in 1944 when her husband, Mr. Harold Stevens, became Headmaster of the Modern School. Mrs. Stevens was Girl Guide Commissioner for Bungay and district for several years, and served for three years from 1949 as President of Bungay Women's Institute. An active member of the Bungay Players, she was also for many years a member of the town's Youth Employment Panel. She was appointed to the Town Trust as a Foundation Feoffee in 1951, and in 1955 to the Nursing Institute Committee.

The third woman to serve as Town Reeve, Mrs. Stevens unfortunately became ill early in her year of office, and many of her engagements were carried out by her husband. She died on 22 August 1971.

1960-61
Major WALTER HUNT WORTLEY, M.R.C.V.S.

Born on 28 July 1891 in Methwold, and educated at Bury St. Edmunds, he was articled to a Downham Market veterinary surgeon before training at the Royal Veterinary College, London, where he qualified in 1914. At the outbreak of war, he joined the Army Veterinary Corps, and was mentioned in dispatches. Demobilized in 1919 with the rank of Captain, he took a veterinary practice at Bungay.

For several years an honorary member of the Eastern Counties Veterinary Society and its 1933 President, he was also an examiner for the Royal College of Veterinary Surgeons. He had a long association with the Waveney Harriers, and belonged to the Bungay and District Branch of the British Legion; he was promoted a Major between the two World Wars. Twice a widower, he had two daughters by his first marriage.

Major Wortley died in office on 6 November 1961, and his Deputy, Mr. Neville Coe, administered the Town Trust for the remaining month of his term. The Town Dinner was cancelled.

1961-62, 1978-79
JACK FREDERICK KEIGHTLEY

Born on 26 January 1915 at Clapton, London, he moved at an early age to North London and was educated at Noel Park Council School at Wood Green. Following some years with a firm making gas lamps, he joined in 1937 the staff of Noakes Bros., who the following year became amalgamated with Richard Clay & Co. Ltd. From 1940, Mr. Keightley served for six years in the Army, including duty in Northern Ireland and Greece, being demobilized with the rank of Captain. He came with his wife Gladys and their son (two further sons and twin daughters were later born to them) in 1946 to Bungay, where he became Bindery Office Manager at the Chaucer Press.

He was elected in 1950 to Bungay Urban District Council, becoming one of its representatives on the Town Trust seven years later. He was appointed a Foundation Feoffee in 1961, and became Town Reeve later the same year. Mr. Keightley was for many years Leader of the Methodist Youth Club at Bungay, Senior Steward of the local circuit, and a local preacher.

Seventeen years after his first term of office, Mr. Keightley again became Town Reeve. During this second term he retired from the Chaucer Press, and attended the Enthronement in St. Edmundsbury Cathedral of the new Bishop of St. Edmundsbury and Ipswich.

Mr. Keightley died on 16 March 1993.

Mrs. VERA STEVENS
Town Reeve
1959-60

Major W. H. WORTLEY
Town Reeve
1960-61

Photograph by courtesy of Eastern Daily Press

JACK KEIGHTLEY
Town Reeve
1961-62 & 1978-79
with Mrs. Gladys Keightley
and guests, including the Rt. Hon. James Prior, M.P. (3rd left)
at the Town Dinner, 1962

CECIL HARRIS
Town Reeve
1962-63

Mrs. LILIAN TRAFFORD
Town Reeve
1963-64 & 1975-76

RONALD DUHY
Town Reeve
1964-65 & 1965-66

REGINALD McDANIEL
Town Reeve
1966-67 & 1999-2000

1962-63
CECIL HARRY HARRIS

Born on 27 August 1900 at Falcon Lane, Ditchingham, he was educated at Wingfield Street Council School, Bungay. Following service with the Royal Fusiliers in the 1914-18 war, in 1919 he became an apprentice in the plumbing, decorating and water-engineering business begun by his grandfather in Bridge Street, taking over when his father died in 1937. He was active in the Fire Service, and joined the East Suffolk Special Constabulary at the beginning of the Second World War.

He was elected to Bungay Urban District Council in 1948, becoming its Chairman from 1959 to 1961, in which year he was appointed a Foundation Feoffee. A former President of Bungay Rotary Club, he was a member of the Bungay and District Branch of the British Legion, and a keen supporter of Norwich City Football Club.

During his year as Town Reeve, he opened the new swimming pool at the Primary School, and attended the opening by Lilias Rider Haggard of the Bungay Museum.

Mr. Harris and his wife, Eva, had two daughters. He died on 7 April 1970.

1963-64, 1975-76
Mrs. LILIAN IRENE TRAFFORD

Miss Lilian Lundie was born on 1 March 1904 at Melton, and educated at the village's Council School, and later at Leiston Grammar School. She married Mr. Donald Trafford in 1940, having one son. Following teaching appointments in her home village and at Woodbridge and Gosbeck, Mrs. Trafford was appointed in 1944 as Headmistress of Bungay Primary School. She served for several years as the representative of primary teachers on the East Suffolk Education Committee, and was President of two local branches of the National Union of Teachers. She served Bungay Women's Institute as President, and Beccles and District Business and Professional Women's Club as Vice-President, also being active in many other organizations in East Suffolk.

Mrs. Trafford, who sponsored the Cub movement in Bungay, did much to promote interest in folk-dancing, for which she was known throughout the county.

A Foundation Feoffee since 1961, she was the fourth woman to become Town Reeve. During her year of office she made a river trip from Bungay to Beccles with other local dignitaries, prior to the closure of navigation along part of the route. She also attended the first meeting of the Court of the University of East Anglia.

Mrs. Trafford retired as Headmistress of Bungay Primary School in 1968. Twelve years after first becoming Town Reeve, she was appointed to the office again. Her second term marked International Women's Year, and was celebrated by a Gala Concert at Bungay High School, in which many local performers took part. Also during the year, at a service at the former Congregational Church, she unveiled a plaque commemorating the formation of Emmanuel Church (United Reformed and Methodist).

Mrs. Trafford's 100th birthday in 2004 was celebrated by a Feoffees' lunch and a reunion of her former colleagues and pupils (see p.100). She died just over a year later, aged 101, on 13 April 2005.

1964-65, 1965-66
RONALD STANLEY ALBERT DUHY, J.P.

Born on 19 July 1912 at Stoke Newington, he joined the London office of Richard Clay & Sons, Ltd., in 1933, and in 1952, having been appointed Assistant Secretary, came to Bungay with his wife, Olive, and their son and daughter. He was promoted as Secretary to the Chaucer Press in 1965, while in office as Town Reeve.

Elected to Bungay Urban District Council in 1955, he served as its Chairman from 1961 to 1963, and in the same capacity to the successor Town Council in 1974. The Council elected him a member of the Town Trust. He has served both the Cherry Tree Angling Club and Bungay Bowls Club as President, and for one year held the same position with the Suffolk County Amalgamated Angling Association. A Magistrate and a General Commissioner of Income Tax, he served Bungay Rotary Club as President and Treasurer.

As Town Reeve, Mr. Duhy attended the 400th Anniversary celebrations of Bungay Grammar School, of which he was a Governor.

At the Town Meeting in December 1965, the Senior Feoffee, Mr. Ronald Wightman, announced that the Feoffees had unanimously asked Mr. Duhy to remain in office for a further year. During this second term, his status on the Town Trust was elevated to that of Foundation Feoffee. Also during this year, Mr. Duhy led the procession at the Installation of the new Chancellor of the University of East Anglia.

Mr. Duhy retired from the Town Trust in 2004 and now lives at Poringland.

1966-67, 1999-2000
REGINALD GEORGE McDANIEL, M.P.S.

Born on 13 November 1926 at Bungay, he was educated at St. Mary's School and Bungay Grammar School, proceeding to the Chelsea School of Pharmacy, where he met his wife, Jacqueline - they have three sons and a daughter. In 1953, he returned as a qualified pharmacist to the Bungay business of his father, later becoming Managing Director.

A member of Bungay Rotary Club and its President in 1961-62, he was also for some years Secretary to the Grammar School Old Students' Association. A keen sportsman, he is particularly interested in sailing, fishing and shooting. He was appointed a Foundation Feoffee in 1961.

The highlight of his first term of office as Town Reeve was a fête held in the Castle grounds to raise funds for the St. Mary's Church Bells Appeal.

Mr. McDaniel took office for the second time when he was appointed in December 1999 to be Town Reeve for the Millennium Year – the interval of thirty-three years between his two terms of office is by far the longest on record! As part of the Festival held during the year, Mr. McDaniel and the Town

Mayor headed a parade through the town, which was followed by the Opening of the Castle Centre and the unveiling of a model of Bungay in mediaeval times. As Town Reeve, Mr. McDaniel held a ball in the Castle grounds in support of the funding of beds for Bungay and District residents at All Hallows Hospital.

1967-68
JOHN EDWARD WILLIAM GIBBS

Born on 31 January 1902 at Flixton, into a farming family, he grew up at Wortwell and attended school in Harleston. He started work at the age of thirteen as a junior clerk in the Bungay office of Mr. Percy Sprake (Town Reeve 1953-54); he was self-taught in acquiring all the skill and knowledge necessary to fulfil the positions he was to hold. Mr. Gibbs, who married Miss Florence Betts in 1928, having two sons, was appointed Assistant Clerk to the Bungay Urban District Council in 1939, and Clerk in 1950. He also served as Chief Financial Officer for Bungay for thirty years, and was appointed to the Town Trust as a Foundation Feoffee in 1967. A fortnight after his retirement the same year, he was elected as the Bungay representative on the East Suffolk County Council, and became Town Reeve soon afterwards.

A former President of Bungay Rotary Club and a member of the Eastern Regional Sports Development Council, Mr. Gibbs was in 1945 appointed a Deacon of Bungay Congregational Church, which he also served as Treasurer and Secretary, and as a lay-preacher.

During his year of office as Town Reeve, he opened 'Fairlands', the East Suffolk County Council specially-designed home for old folk at Bungay.

Mr. Gibbs died on 14 August 1988.

1968-69
ANTHONY REGINALD HOOD, A.I.B.

Born on 12 March 1926 at Loddon, he was educated at Loddon Primary School, and from 1938 to 1943 at Bungay Grammar School. His various posts of increasing responsibility with Barclay's Bank, interrupted by his National Service in the Royal Air Force, included a two-and-a-half-year spell at the Bungay branch, to which he returned in 1966 as Manager. Having been elected to Bungay Urban District Council and become a Councillor Feoffee in 1968, he was appointed Town Reeve the same year. In his first week of office, he opened Bungay's new Telephone Exchange, and later in the year he took part in a television debate on the office of Town Reeve and its powers. The Town Reeve's appeal for the St. John's Ambulance raised almost £1,500, and a new ambulance was handed over within six months.

Mr. Hood served as Treasurer of the Bungay branch of the Red Cross Association, and on the committee of the local branch of the Lowestoft Division Conservative Association. He was a member of the Bungay and Waveney Valley Golf Club, and was a keen cricketer. He and his wife, Elizabeth, have a son and a daughter.

Mr. Hood was Vice-Chairman of the Waveney District Council before leaving Bungay in 1975 to pursue his career with Barclays Bank as Manager of the St. Stephen's Branch in Norwich – he retired in 1984.

Mr. Hood represented Sprowston on Norfolk County Council for eight years and was Chairman of the Fire Committee from 1982 to 1985.

Mr. and Mrs. Hood now live at Bramerton.

1969-70. 1970-71
HERBERT FRANK WHYTE

Born on 17 November 1900 in Bungay, he was educated at the Wingfield Street School. He married in 1920, and with his wife, Doris, ran a confectionery shop in Ipswich for three years, returning to Bungay to run a newsagent's and stationer's shop in Broad Street. In 1954 he moved the business to Earsham Street, where his mother had run a confectioner's since 1911.

He was elected in 1948 as an independent member of Bungay Urban District Council, almost always topping the poll in subsequent elections, and serving as Chairman from 1957 to 1959. He had also been appointed in 1948 as a Councillor Feoffee.

For many years he was a great champion of Bungay Town Football Club, serving as both Secretary and Treasurer, and a senior member of the Bungay Earl of Bigod Lodge of the Royal Antedeluvian Order of Buffalos. A committee member of Bungay and District Chamber of Trade, he was also a Manager of Bungay County Primary School.

Early in his first year of office he and his wife, who had six sons and a daughter, celebrated their Golden Wedding.

At the Town Meeting in December 1970, Mr. Whyte announced that the Feoffees had asked him to remain in office for a second term. He died on 27 April 1980.

1971-72
JOHN CHARLES HAYLOCK MAIDMENT,
M.D., B.S. (Lond.), M.R.C.S., L.R.C.P. (Eng.)

Born on 8 May 1917 at Harleston, the son of a doctor in the town, he was educated at Taverham Hall, Norwich, and Haileybury College, proceeding to train for the medical profession at the London Hospital, where he qualified in 1940. Following a period of four years in the R.A.F., much of which was spent in the Far East, and post-graduate work in London, he returned to Harleston. Shortly afterwards, in 1951, he moved to Bungay to join Dr. P. G. Levick (Town Reeve 1956-57) in medical practice, later becoming his partner. Dr. Maidment and his wife, Morag, had three sons.

The Medical Officer of All Hallows County Hospital, Ditchingham, Dr. Maidment, who became a Foundation Feoffee in 1967, marked his term of office as Town Reeve by raising £23,000 as the result of an appeal on the occasion of its Centenary, which fell during the year. Some years later, he became the Senior Partner in Bungay's new combined Medical Practice, having rebuilt his former surgery.

Dr. Maidment died on 17 January 2005, while visiting relatives in Australia.

JOHN GIBBS
Town Reeve
1967-68

ANTHONY HOOD
Town Reeve
1968-69

HERBERT WHYTE
Town Reeve
1969-70 & 1970-71

Dr. CHARLES MAIDMENT
Town Reeve
1971-72

BURTON NURSEY
Town Reeve
1972-73

Dr. WYNDHAM JORDAN
Town Reeve
1973-74

IVOR BALDWIN
Town Reeve
1974-75

MICHAEL BELCHER
Town Reeve
1976-77
with the outgoing Town Reeve,
Mrs. Lilian Trafford,
at the Town Meeting, 1976

1972-73
SAMUEL BURTON NURSEY

Burton Nursey was born at Bungay on 2 July 1919, and educated at Bracondale School, Norwich. Following a period of practical business training in Ipswich, he returned to Bungay to join his mother in the family sheepskin business of Nursey & Son, Ltd., eventually becoming its Managing Director. He resigned from this rôle in 1997, becoming the firm's Life Chairman.

He was a member of the Institute of Directors from 1966, and Chairman of the Leather Clothing Manufacturers of Great Britain for some years. He was instrumental in the founding of Bungay and District Chamber of Trade, of the town's Young Conservatives, and of Suffolk Exporters. For some years a Bungay U.D.C. representative on the Town Trust, he became a Foundation Feoffee in 1967, resigning in 1999.

The first person to follow a mother (Mrs. Hilda Nursey, 1955-56) as Town Reeve, Mr. Nursey during his year of office attended with his wife, Bridget, the wedding of their only son. He also successfully concerned himself with the Trust's financial affairs.

1973-74
WYNDHAM MACKRAY JORDAN,
M.A., B.M., B.Chir. (Oxon.), D.R.C.O.G.

Born on 1 August 1926 at Kuala Lumpur, Malaya, he was educated at Winchester College, New College, Oxford, and the London Hospital Medical College, where he qualified in 1951. Between periods as a House Surgeon in London and Solihull, where he specialized in obstetrics, he served for two years as Captain in the R.A.M.C. in Egypt and Malta. Following a year in general practice near Chesterfield, he came to Bungay in 1957 as partner to Dr. Hugh Cane (Town Reeve 1957-58). Dr. Jordan became a Foundation Feoffee in 1967; he and his wife, Elizabeth, had a son and three daughters.

A member of the British Legion and the Bungay Society, and of the Board of Management of All Hallows Hospital, Ditchingham, Dr. Jordan was the Lay Chairman of Beccles and South Elmham Deanery Synod, and the Secretary and Organizer of Bungay and District Christian Aid.

During his term of office as Town Reeve, which saw the reorganization of local government, he inaugurated the new ambulance of the St. John Ambulance Brigade. The St. Edmund's Almshouses in Outney Road were completely modernized during the year, and re-opened by Earl Stradbroke, Lord Lieutenant of Suffolk. Also during the year, Dr. Jordan presided at a meeting to inaugurate the Bungay and District Branch of the Lions' Club.

Dr. Jordan died on 27 March 1996.

1974-75
IVOR GERALD BALDWIN

Born on 15 December 1926 at Woodton, and educated in the village, he was apprenticed as a compositor with Richard Clay at Bungay in February

1941. After volunteering for the Royal Air Force in 1943 he was transferred the following year to the Army, and served with the 6th Airborne Division in Palestine, and later with the British Military Mission to Greece. Resuming his career in Bungay, he eventually took charge of the Computer Filmsetting and Teletypesetting Departments after a study tour taking in the East Coast and Central U.S.A. Moving into the town upon marriage, he and his wife, Whybra, had two daughters.

Formerly a member of the Bungay Urban District Council, which appointed him to the Town Trust in 1971, he continued with the successor Town Council, and became Town Reeve six months after its creation. He became a Foundation Feoffee in 1979. Mr. Baldwin was Secretary and Treasurer of Woodton Football and Cricket Clubs as well as being a playing member. He was also a useful golf and tennis player, and took part in many local sporting events. After election to the U.D.C. he became actively engaged in many local charities as well as being a Board Member of All Hallows Hospital and a School Governor.

During his year as Town Reeve he appeared on television programmes for both BBC and ITV, giving interviews on the history of the office. He organized a Charity Ball for All Hallows Hospital and a party for the Muscular Dystrophy Society, opened six fêtes and attended many civic and charitable functions throughout the Waveney Valley.

Mr. Baldwin retired from work in 1991 after more than fifty years. He was a member of Bungay Town Council for seventeen years and of the Scott Charity for twenty-five years, including ten as Chairman.

Mr. Baldwin died on 19 May 2001 while tending the family graves at Woodton.

1976-77
MICHAEL PERCY BELCHER

Born on 26 November 1926 at Southwold, he was educated at Norwich School and, following four years in the Royal Navy, at Norwich City College. He married in 1959 Miss Diana Heyner of Beccles, having two sons and a daughter.

He came to Bungay in 1964 on the purchase of T. Simons, Ltd., by the family firm of Belchers Motor Group, Ltd., of which he later became Managing Director. He was President of Bungay Rotary Club in the same year that his father held the position in the Southwold Club. Elected to the Town Council in 1976, he became a Councillor Feoffee and Town Reeve, all in the same year.

Mr. Belcher's was a particularly historic year of office, seeing the Queen's Silver Jubilee, in commemoration of which Mr. Belcher added a further medallion to the chain of office, and in Bungay the centenaries of Richard Clay (The Chaucer Press) Ltd., and Bungay Primary School, and the 400th Anniversary of the Black Dog legend of 1577. Mr. Belcher also attended as Town Reeve the dedication of the former Methodist Church building as Headquarters of the St. John Ambulance Brigade.

Mr. Belcher is now Chairman of the Markets Committee.

1977-78
DOUGLAS RAYMOND VERNON CROCKETT, M.C.

Born on 27 July 1923 at Gravesend, Kent, and educated at the Grammar School there, he came in 1941 to join his family, who had been evacuated to Bungay. Enlisting the same year in the Army, he was later commissioned in the Black Watch, and was awarded the Military Cross. Returning to Bungay, he joined the Accounts Department of Richard Clay (The Chaucer Press) Ltd. in 1947, and was for many years Secretary of the Chaucer Club, and an active member of Bungay Players.

He was elected to Bungay Town Council in 1976, and became a Councillor Feoffee the same year. Following the death of his first wife, Florence, Mr. Crockett married his second wife, Brenda, in 1972. He has five sons and a daughter and two step-children.

Early in his year of office as Town Reeve, Mr. Crockett opened Bungay's new Group Practice Surgery.

Mr. Crockett resigned from the Town Trust on moving to Beccles. He died on 6 April 2007.

1979-80
GEORGE WILLIAM JOHN FRANKLIN, D.F.C., M.A.

He was born on 18 September 1918 at Crowborough, Sussex, and educated at Lewes County Grammar School. After some years in accountancy and company secretarial work, he served with the Royal Air Force in Europe and the Far East for the duration of the 1939-45 war, and was awarded the Distinguished Flying Cross in 1944. After the war he studied for an honours degree at Fitzwilliam College, Cambridge, and went on to teach history and geography at Loughborough and Whitehaven Grammar Schools.

Mr. Franklin came to Bungay in 1961 to succeed Mr. D.L. Hewitt (twice Town Reeve) as Headmaster of the Grammar School, guiding it through its development in a new building, first as a co-educational establishment, and later as a comprehensive school. A keen historian, Mr. Franklin was for two years Chairman of the Bungay Society, and was also Senior Churchwarden at Holy Trinity Church.

Mr. Franklin's son was tragically drowned in a rowing accident in 1969; he and his wife, Dorothy, also had a daughter. Appointed in 1978 as a Foundation Feoffee, a memorable highlight of his year as Town Reeve was the visit to Bungay of Brian Johnston and the BBC 'Down Your Way' team.

Mr. Franklin died on 23 October 1997.

1980-81, 1989-90, 2005-06
Mrs. MARY KENT

Miss Mary Worth was born on 21 January 1922 in Cork, Éire, and at the age of three moved with her family from Bolton, Lancashire, to Great Yarmouth, where she was educated at St. Louis Convent High School. Having done war service in the A.T.S., in 1944 she married Mr. William Kent, an architect born in Czechoslovakia; they have four sons.

Having travelled the world in pursuit of Mr. Kent's career, they settled in 1966 in Bungay, where Mrs. Kent four years later became Secretary to the Personnel Director at Richard Clay & Co. She was elected to the recently reformed Bungay Town Council, which she later served as its first woman Chairman, also becoming one of its representatives on the Town Trust, as well as County Councillor for the town, all in the same year, 1976.

The fifth woman to serve as Town Reeve, Mrs. Kent marked the wedding of H.R.H. the Prince of Wales and Lady Diana Spencer during her year of office by the addition of a further commemorative medallion to the chain of office. The event was also marked by the planting of a tree on the Drift.

Nine years after first becoming Town Reeve, Mrs. Kent was appointed to serve a second term, during which a Festival was held celebrating the Tercentenary of the Butter Cross.

Mrs. Kent retired from the County Council and Bungay Town Council in 1989, having served the latter for a second time as Chairman four years previously. Later, she also relinquished her involvement with the Citizens' Advice Bureau, the Great Yarmouth and Waveney Health Authority, and as a Governor of all Bungay Schools.

In 2005, Mrs. Kent became Town Reeve for the third time – such a situation had not occurred for over sixty years, and it was the first time ever that a lady had been Town Reeve three times. During the year a Dinner with entertainment was held at Bungay Community Centre in celebration of the 80th Birthday of Her Majesty Queen Elizabeth II.

1981-82
RICHARD WALTER MIGHELL MONKS, M.R.C.V.S.

He was born on 1 March 1924 at Herne Hill, Kent, and educated at Cranleigh School, Surrey. Following his R.A.F. service and training at the Royal Veterinary College, London, he came to Bungay as a newly-qualified veterinary surgeon in 1952, to work with Major W.H. Wortley (Town Reeve 1960-61), in whose practice he became a partner four years later.

Mr. Monks, who became a Foundation Feoffee in 1978, was at the time of his appointment as Town Reeve also Chairman of Ilketshall St. Margaret Parish Meeting and Chairman of the Governors of Ilketshall St. Lawrence Primary School, having also served as Chairman to Ilketshall St. Margaret Village Hall Committee, Ilketshall St. Margaret Town Estate Charity, and Beccles and Bungay Riding Club.

As Town Reeve, Mr. Monks revived the Wingfield Dinner and Sermon which had lapsed since 1938. Also during his term of office, he attended the opening of Bungay High School Sports Hall, and presented a gavel and stand to the Town Trust; he became its representative on the Scott Charity. He and his wife, Jean, had two sons and a daughter.

Mr. Monks died on 5 April 1996.

DOUGLAS CROCKETT
Town Reeve
1977-78
with Mrs. Brenda Crockett

JOHN FRANKLIN
Town Reeve
1979-80

Mrs. MARY KENT
Town Reeve
1980-81, 1989-90 & 2005-06

RICHARD MONKS
Town Reeve
1981-82
with Mrs. Jean Monks

COLIN RICHARDSON
Town Reeve
1982-83
with Mrs. Janet Richardson

HARALD PULFORD
Town Reeve
1983-84
with Mrs. Margaret Pulford

PAUL WOODCOCK
Town Reeve
1984-85

Mrs. CICELY SMITH
Town Reeve
1985-86

1982-83
DAVID COLIN CHARLES RICHARDSON

Colin Richardson was born on 31 December 1931 at West Mersea in Essex, and moved with his family to Beccles in 1938, attending Bungay Grammar School from 1943 to 1949. Following his National Service in the Royal Air Force he in 1952 joined the staff of Richard Clay (The Chaucer Press), becoming a group account controller in the Bible Division; he retired in 1995. A keen sportsman, he met his wife, Janet, at a Beccles Hockey Club dance - they married in 1956, living firstly in Ditchingham and then in Bungay. They have a son and a daughter and five grandchilden.

Mr. Richardson was appointed to the Town Trust in 1978 as a Foundation Feoffee. He also served on Bungay Town Council for twenty years, becoming Chairman in 1980 and again in 1991. For fifteen years he was a member of Waveney District Council, being Chairman in 1986-87. He was a Governor of Bungay High School for thirty years, including serving as Chairman; he has also served on the steering committee of the town's Shell Youth Club, and been a Church Councillor at Emmanuel Church, Bungay, of which he and his wife have been members for over fifty years.

Two of Mr. Richardson's special guests at the Town Dinner over which he presided at the end of his year of office were Dr. Christopher Cook, M.A., the Editor of Pear's Cyclopaedia, and Mr. D. L. Hewitt, M.A. (twice Town Reeve), his former Headmaster.

1983-84
HARALD RHYS GORDON PULFORD, M.B.E.

Born on 4 May 1933 at Woodbridge, he started work at a bakery in Harleston before joining the forces, serving in the Royal Army Medical Corps during the Korean War. He joined Nursey & Son at Bungay in 1954 as a cutter and shop assistant, and progressed to become the firm's Production Manager, retiring in 1998. He and his wife, Margaret, were married in 1962.

First elected to Bungay Urban District Council in 1969, he became Chairman of the successor Town Council in 1977, retiring in 1995. Originally elected to the Town Trust by the Council in 1969, he was appointed a Foundation Feoffee in 1982, and served as Chairman of the Trust's Almshouse Branch for four years, from 1980 to 1983. A founder member of the Association of Friends of All Hallows Hospital, Ditchingham, he was for six years the Chairman of its Fund-Raising Committee. Retiring as Chairman of the Association in 2004, he became its new Honorary President.

As Town Reeve, Mr. Pulford launched an appeal for £8,000 for repairs to the Butter Cross. Also during his term of office, in 1984, the Charity Commission's new scheme for the administration of the Town Trust was implemented.

A founder Trustee and Honorary Secretary of Bungay Medical Centre Charitable Trust, Mr. Pulford was awarded the M.B.E. in the New Year's Honours List in 2000 for services to the Town of Bungay.

1984-85
JOHN RICHARD PAUL WOODCOCK

Born on 3 February 1925 at Aberavon and educated at Alconbury Church of England School, Paul Woodcock served an apprenticeship as a motor mechanic until 1943, prior to three years in the Royal Naval Air Service. Joining the wine merchants' firm of Hunter and Oliver in 1947 as a driver-salesman, he became Deputy Manager at Huntingdon, and was appointed Manager of the Bungay branch in 1962; the firm was taken over in 1968 by Peter Dominic. He retired in 1990.

Mr. Woodcock, who was appointed a Foundation Feoffee in 1982, was District Commissioner of the Waveney Valley Scouts and a Governor of Bungay Middle School. He and his wife, Jean, had one son.

In the summer of their year of office, Mr. and Mrs. Woodcock were present at the Royal Visit to Lowestoft of the Queen and Prince Philip.

Mr. Woodcock died on 11 August 2003.

1985-86
Mrs. CICELY MARY SMITH

Miss Cicely Coe was born on 13 April 1929 at 17, St. John's Road, Bungay; her grandparents, and later parents, ran a grocery and hardware business in Bridge Street. Following her education at St. Mary's School in Earsham Street, she worked in local government for many years, and in 1969 married a colleague, Mr. Harry Smith.

She was elected in 1968 to Bungay Urban District Council, serving for three years, and in 1976 to the Town Council, which she served as Chairman in 1981-82. She was elected as a Councillor Feoffee in 1976. The first Secretary of the Bungay Society, and its Chairman from 1982 to 1984, she was also a founder member and Secretary of the Friends of St. Mary's Church. The Chairman of Bungay Women Conservatives and of the Waveney Constituency Women's Committee, she was also a member of the Women's Royal Voluntary Service, and a Governor of Bungay First School, a Trustee of the Eliza Dreyer Homes and of the Bungay Museum.

The sixth woman, and the first of Bungay birth, to serve as Town Reeve, Mrs. Smith during her year of office attended the Centenary Reunion of her old school, and unveiled a commemorative plaque on the wall of the former St. Mary's School. The year also saw progress being made towards the formation of a Trust to take over the ownership of Bungay Castle from the Duke of Norfolk.

Mrs. Smith died on 11 December 1991.

1986-87
Lt.-Col. ROSEMARY MARTIN, R.R.C., S.R.N., S.C.M.

The niece of Mr. Ronald Wightman (three times Town Reeve), she was born on 22 January 1930 in London and educated latterly at St. Mary's School, Bungay. Having undertaken her nursing and midwifery training at the Norfolk and Norwich Hospital and in London, Miss Martin joined Queen Alexandra's Royal Army Nursing Corps, serving between 1956 and 1981 in East Africa, Mauritius, with the British Army on the Rhine, and in Malaya, Singapore, Borneo, Cyprus and Hong Kong.

Returning to Bungay, she has been the W.R.V.S. Local Organizer since 1982, when she also became a member of the P.C.C. of Holy Trinity Church, serving for five years. In the same year, she was also appointed to the Town Trust as a Foundation Feoffee.

Miss Martin became the seventh woman Town Reeve in 1986, and the first single woman to hold the office – it was also the first time that one lady had directly succeeded another. Miss Martin chose her friend, Miss Tess Rees, as her supporter, and with her predecessor, Mrs. Cicely Smith, as her deputy, it was the first time in history that all three positions had been in female hands!

During her term of office, Miss Martin attended a service commemorating the centenary year of the Bungay St. John Ambulance; the year also saw the opening of the Bigod Way and the establishment of Bungay Castle Trust Ltd., with charitable status being granted.

1987-88
JOHN VICTOR PALIN

He was born in Coulsdon, Surrey, on 27 November 1934, and moved with his family to Bungay, his mother's home town, in 1938. Educated at Bungay schools, he worked at Clay's Ltd., as a printer's reader and copy preparer for thirty-six years after leaving Bungay Grammar School.

Since first being elected in 1967, Mr. Palin has continuously served the former Bungay Urban District Council and the present Bungay Town Council, of which he was Chairman in 1976 and 1990, and Town Mayor in 2003. He was elected to Waveney District Council in 1982 and served as a Bungay representative for thirteen years. He married Miss Pauline Newby in Bungay in 1960, and they have a daughter and a son.

Appointed to the Town Trust in 1968 as a Councillor Feoffee, he was later made a Foundation Feoffee in 1998. He has served on the Friends of All Hallows Hospital committee for over twenty years and is a member of Bungay Area Community Transport committee, a Trustee of the Eliza Dreyer Homes and Bungay United Charities, and for thirteen years was a member of Suffolk Valuation Tribunal.

During Mr. Palin's year of office, the 300th Anniversary of the Great Fire of Bungay was commemorated by a firework display at the Castle, the publication of a book by Mr. Terry Reeve, and a television documentary.

1988-89
DESMOND PERCY SCARLE, M.B.E., I.R.R.V.

Born on 7 April 1925 at Oulton Broad, and educated at Lowestoft Grammar School, he entered local government in January 1942 in the Finance Department at Lowestoft Town Hall, and remained in the service of various local authorities in Suffolk until he succeeded Mr. John Gibbs (Town Reeve 1967-68) as Clerk and Chief Financial Officer to Bungay Urban District Council in 1966 – the only break was for war service in the Royal Navy as a Sub-Lieutenant R.N.V.R. In 1947, he married Miss Audrey Jude, also of Oulton Broad, and they have one son and two grandchildren.

Following re-organisation of local government in 1974, Mr. Scarle was appointed Assistant Treasurer to Waveney District Council until he retired in 1988, having been made a Foundation Feoffee in 1982. He was appointed Clerk to Bungay Charities and a member of Waveney Valley Drainage Board in 1967, and since retirement has been made Chairman of Suffolk Valuation Tribunal, and also of Suffolk Agriculture Dwelling House Advisory Committee. He is currently Chairman of the Finance Committee of the Town Trust, a position he has held for a number of years.

During his year of office as Town Reeve he carried out extensive improvements to the Castle Hills, and attended the official opening of the Citizens' Advice Bureau by Earl Ferrers. However, the highlight of his year came when he was invested with the M.B.E. by Her Majesty The Queen at Buckingham Palace, for services to the community in the Waveney District.

1990-91
GRAHAM JOHN MAY, B.Sc.

Born on 9 April 1939 at Gillingham, Kent, he was educated in Lancashire and Cheshire, where he was Head Boy at Wirral Grammar School. He gained his Degree in Mathematics at Manchester University, and a Diploma in Physical Education at Carnegie College, Leeds.

Following teaching posts at Bungay and Lowestoft, Mr. May was at the Island School, Hong Kong, for a long time before returning to Bungay High School. He and his wife, Patricia, who have a son and a daughter and five grandchildren, also ran the school boarding house at 'Dunelm' for twelve years until its closure.

A Past President of Bungay Rotary Club, Mr. May is also Chairman of the Suffolk Professional Association of Teachers and the Suffolk Schools' Cycling Association, and he was appointed to the Town Trust as the last full Foundation Feoffee in 1984. A keen sportsman, he has played football, rugby, cricket and hockey for local clubs, and ran the Bungay Black Dog Half-Marathon as Town Reeve.

Mr. May enjoyed a particularly eventful year of office – he welcomed the Princess Royal to Bungay (see p. 98), appeared with Sir Harry Secombe in Anglia Television's 'Highway' programme, took part in a Gala Concert at Hunstanton and opened the extension of the Bungay Group Medical Practice at his old home in Lower Olland Street. The Bungay Bigod Festival was celebrated, and the year also saw the revival of the historic Wingfield Dinner.

Miss ROSEMARY MARTIN
Town Reeve
1986-87

JOHN PALIN
Town Reeve
1987-88

DESMOND SCARLE
Town Reeve
1988-89

GRAHAM MAY
Town Reeve
1990-91
with Mrs. Patricia May

COLIN HANCY
Town Reeve
1991-92
with Mrs. Mary-Jane Hancy

Mrs. DIANA BELCHER
Town Reeve
1992-93 & 2003-04

PETER MORROW
Town Reeve
1993-94

JIM JERVIS
Town Reeve
1994-95
with Mrs. Marlene Jervis

The Town Reeve's fund-raising efforts were mainly directed towards the Bungay High School Library Appeal and All Hallows Hospital, Ditchingham.

Mr. May retired from Bungay High School in 2001, and in 2007 is for the second time President of Bungay Rotary Club.

1991-92
COLIN ROY HANCY

He was born on 17 December 1946 at Outney Common End, Bungay, and educated at the town's Primary and Secondary Modern Schools and Lowestoft Technical College. After serving an electrical apprenticeship at Beccles, he joined a Dutch oilfield-drilling company and spent twelve years working in the North Sea, Africa and the Middle East.

Returning to Bungay in 1980 to join his father's caravan park business, he has a bottle gas franchise and a rowing-boat hire and camping park business. He married his second wife, Mary-Jane, also Bungay-born, in California, U.S.A., in 1990. They each have a daughter and a son.

Elected in 1983 to Bungay Town Council, which he served as Chairman in 1987, Mr. Hancy was appointed to the Town Trust in 1984 as a Councillor Feoffee. He served as a Governor of Bungay Middle School and is Chairman of Bungay Castle Trust.

Mr. Hancy, the first Town Reeve to have been born since the Second World War, became a grandfather during his year of office – there were at that time five generations of his family all living.

During his year of office, Mr. Hancy attended the opening of a new wing at Bungay Middle School, and the laying of the foundations of the new Bungay Library. He also made a civic visit to H.M.S. Brave at Harwich, presided over the Bungay Riverside Festival, and addressed the National Association of City and Town Sheriffs of England and Wales.

A member of the Rotary Club of Bungay, Mr. Hancy was President in 2004-05.

1992-93, 2003-04
Mrs. DIANA HAMILTON BELCHER, S.R.N.

Miss Diana Heyner was born on 7 November 1937 at Berkhampstead, Herts., and educated at the Sir John Leman School, Beccles. Following her training at the Middlesex Hospital in London, she nursed at Southwold Hospital. In 1959 she married Mr. Michael Belcher (Town Reeve 1976-77); they have three children.

Moving to Bungay with her family in 1964, Mrs. Belcher worked for many years as a Company Secretary for her husband's family business, returning to nursing in 1984. She was appointed to the Town Trust as a Foundation Feoffee in 1978.

The eighth woman Town Reeve, Mrs. Belcher became the first person to take office having previously served as Consort – never before had a husband and wife both been Town Reeve!

During her year, Mrs. Belcher reinstated the office of Town Crier in Bungay, presided over the Black Dog Festival and donated an ultra-sound machine to the new Physiotherapy Department at All Hallows Hospital, Ditchingham. She was interviewed by BBC TV's "Look East" programme on the office of Town Reeve.

Eleven years later, Mrs. Belcher became Town Reeve for the second time. During this year, she had the honour of hosting a lunch for the Feoffees on the occasion of the 100th Birthday of Mrs. Lilian Trafford (twice Town Reeve) (see p. 100).

1993-94
PETER MORROW, B.A.

An identical twin, he was born on 15 February 1951 at Emsworth, West Sussex, and educated at the Royal Hospital School, Holbrook, and St. Paul's College, Cheltenham. He and his wife, Rachel, moved to Bungay shortly after their marriage in 1974; they have four sons.

Mr. Morrow, who works as a tax consultant for a firm of Norwich solicitors, in 1984 founded Morrow & Co., book publishers, and has published several titles, most of them relating to various aspects of Bungay history.

In 1986 Mr. Morrow became Town Clerk, and he was two years later appointed to the Town Trust as a Councillor Feoffee; he also became Clerk to Bungay Castle Trust. A Trustee of Bungay Museum, and a Governor and former Chairman of Bungay Primary School, he was also a founder member of Bungay Black Dog Marathon and Bungay Black Dog Running Club.

Mr. Morrow's inauguration, when he became the second person to hold concurrently the offices of Town Reeve and Town Clerk, was filmed for BBC TV News. During his year of office, he presided over the Bungay Castle Festival, which celebrated the 700th anniversary of the crenellation of the Castle by Roger Bigod, 5th Earl of Norfolk, and the highlight of which was a mediaeval jousting tourament held on the Castle bailey. Some £4,000 was raised for the Bungay Castle Appeal during the year.

Mr. & Mrs. Morrow held a tea party to celebrate the 90th birthday of Mrs. Lilian Trafford (twice Town Reeve) and hosted a dinner attended by eighteen former Town Reeves.

Mr. Morrow is now Chairman of Bungay United Charities.

1994-95
JAMES HERBERT JERVIS, B.Sc. (Eng.)

Jim Jervis was born on 15 June 1943 at Spixworth, and educated at the Alderman Jex School and the Hewett School, Norwich. He obtained his Degree in Civil Engineering at the City University, London, and a Diploma in Physical Education at Loughborough Colleges.

Mr. Jervis began his teaching career at Earsham Hall School in the year of his marriage, 1967; he and his wife, Marlene have two daughters and two granddaughters.

In 1970 Mr. Jervis was appointed as Head of the P.E. Department of Bungay Grammar School and to teach Physics – he retired on health grounds in 1993. He enjoyed many seasons of club rugby with Norwich and Beccles; a founder member of the Black Dog Running Club and the Bungay Marathon, he is currently President of both. He was also a founder member of Bungay in Bloom, and of the Tourism and Bungay Festival Committees.

Mr. Jervis was elected to Bungay Town Council in 1984, becoming its Chairman in 1988. He was appointed to the Town Trust as a Councillor Feoffee in 1986.

Mr. Jervis's year of office was dominated by the 50th Anniversary celebrations of VE Day and VJ Day and, with the Chairman of the Town Council, he presided over a full programme of events, including parties for war veterans, concerts, races and commemorative services, and the Bungay Festival, celebrating fifty years of peace in the town. Two cast-iron commemorative seats were placed at the Butter Cross. The Centenary of the building of the almshouses in Outney Road by Frederic Smith (four times Town Reeve) was also celebrated during the year.

The Friends of St. Mary's Church were the major beneficiaries of the Town Reeve's fund-raising activites, and now Mr. Jervis is Vice-Chairman of the Friends.

1995-96
PETER DUNCAN SCOTT, M.A. (Ed.), M.I.P.D.

He was born on 8 February 1953 in Bristol and educated at Leeds Modern Grammar School and Leeds University, where he obtained a degree in Textiles and Management Studies.

Mr. Scott spent the early part of his career in the retail trade. He met his wife, Diane, while working in the Lowestoft area – they married in 1977 and lived in Leeds before moving to Bungay in 1985. Mr. Scott is employed as a Contracts Manager for Youth and Adult Training Programmes with Norfolk Learning and Skills Council.

He was elected to Bungay Town Council in 1991, becoming Chairman in 1994. He was appointed as a Councillor Feoffee to the Town Trust in 1992, becoming Town Reeve three years later; he was elected a Foundation Feoffee in 1998.

Mr. Scott was the first Town Reeve to have been born in the reign of Queen Elizabeth II; Her Majesty's 70th Birthday fell during his year of office, and an illuminated scroll was sent to her by the Town Trust to mark the event. During the year Mr. Scott met the Archbishop of Canterbury, Dr. George Carey, at the dedication of the new chapel at Adele House, and assisted with the campaign to retain National Health Service contracts for All Hallows Hospital, Ditchingham. He also served on the committee for the Bungay and District Minibus Appeal.

The carnival procession was restored at the Bungay Festival, and among fund-raising events organised by Mr. and Mrs. Scott was a Town Reeve's Ball held in a marquee in the floodlit grounds of Bungay Castle. Total funds raised for the Town Reeve's Appeal were in excess of £3,500, the main beneficiary being the appeal for an adventure playground at Bungay First School, which Mr. Scott served as a Governor.

1996-97, 2002-03
TERENCE GEORGE REEVE

Terry Reeve was born on 19 April 1943 in Bungay, and educated at St. Mary's School and Bungay Grammar School. He joined Eastern Counties Newspapers as a reporter in 1962, and in the course of his career with the company has been based at its offices in Cromer, King's Lynn, Thetford, Swaffham, Great Yarmouth, Norwich, Beccles and Lowestoft. He is currently Chief Reporter for the Lowestoft Journal, also working on the Eastern Daily Press and various weekly newspapers; he has also written three books on Bungay topics.

Since returning to Bungay in 1985, he has served as Chairman of Bungay Town Football Club, Bungay Primary School governors, the Holy Trinity Church Appeal committee and the Bungay Society. He has also been a Governor of Bungay Middle School and a member of the Parochial Church Council, and is a trustee of Bungay Museum and of the Eliza Dreyer Homes. He was appointed to Bungay Town Trust as a Foundation Feoffee in 1995, becoming 'T. Reeve, Town Reeve' the following year. He has three sons and a daughter.

During an eventful year of office, Mr. Reeve met Her Majesty The Queen in West Norfolk (see p.99) and H.R.H. The Princess Margaret at Somerleyton Hall, but also had the sad task of raising the Bigod flag to half-mast on Bungay Castle following the tragic death of Diana, Princess of Wales, in August 1997; he attended the county memorial service for her at St. Edmundsbury Cathedral and also represented Bungay at many other events, including the institution of the Bishop of St. Edmundsbury and Ipswich.

Mr. Reeve's year of office and the Golden Wedding Anniversary of H.M. The Queen and H.R.H. The Duke of Edinburgh were jointly celebrated with a Gala Concert held at Bungay High School, and proceeds from the Town Reeve's fundraising activites were divided between the 1st Bungay Sea Scouts' 50th Anniversary boathouse project and the Bungay Area Community Minibus fund.

After only six years, Mr. Reeve took office for the second time. During the year, on his 60th Birthday, he married his third wife, Penny, gaining three step-children. With Mrs. Susan Curtis, he was instrumental in setting up the Bungay fund-raising committee of the N.S.P.C.C.; his own fund-raising activities benefitted the Fisher Theatre project and the Bungay and District Sports Association.

1997-98
Mrs. BETTY JOAN WARNES

Miss Betty Honeywood was born on 17 August 1936 in Bungay, but moved into Norfolk at an early age. Following her education at Ditchingham Primary School and the Sir John Leman School, Beccles, she worked at the Bungay and Beccles branches of the Midland Bank.

In 1965 she married Mr. W. John Warnes (son of Mr. Cecil Warnes, Town Reeve 1947-48); they have a daughter and a son.

PETER SCOTT
Town Reeve
1995-96
with Mrs. Diane Scott

TERRY REEVE
Town Reeve
1996-97 & 2002-03

Mrs. BETTY WARNES
Town Reeve
1997-98
with Mr. John Warnes
Photograph by courtesy of E.D.P.

Mrs. ROMA WENT
Town Reeve
1998-99
with Mr. Geoffrey Went

ARTHUR FISHER
Town Reeve
2000-01
with Mrs. Mavis Fisher
at the Town Dinner, 2001

Mrs. SUSAN CURTIS
Town Reeve
2001-02

STEPHEN WENT
Town Reeve
2004-05

Mrs. MAUREEN DAVIES
Town Reeve
2006-07

Mrs. Warnes joined the family company (Warnes & Co.) in 1970, and was elected to Bungay Town Trust as a Foundation Feoffee in 1989.

A Past President of Bungay Chamber of Trade, she is a founder member of Bungay Joint Tourism Committee and the Bungay Society, both of which she served as Treasurer. She is currently Secretary of the Bungay Joint Tourism Committee and also Chairman of the Friends of St. Mary's Church. She was elected to Bungay Town Council in 1995.

Mrs. Warnes became the ninth woman Town Reeve, and the first daughter-in-law of a former incumbent to take office, on the fiftieth anniversary of her father-in-law's nomination in 1947.

During her year of office, Mrs. Warnes was Guest of Honour at a Honeywood Family Convention, held in Bungay and attended by many of her closer and more distant relatives.

Proceeds from the Bungay Festival presided over by Mrs. Warnes as Town Reeve enabled the floodlighting in St. Mary's churchyard to be replaced.

Mrs. Warnes became Mayor of Bungay in 2000, but retired from the Town Council in 2007.

1998-99
Mrs. ROMA HAZEL WENT

Miss Roma Read was born on 24 March 1933 in Bungay, and educated at Bungay Primary School, Bungay Modern School and Norwich Secretarial College. Her parents for many years ran the Horse and Groom Public House in Broad Street.

She started work in the office at Charles Marston Flour Mills in 1947, transferring two years later to Vitovis Animal Feeds at Ellingham Mill. She left work in 1956, having married Mr. Geoffrey Went the previous year; they have three sons.

Mrs. Went was elected to Bungay Town Council in 1995, and appointed the following year to the Town Trust as a Councillor Feoffee, becoming Town Reeve after a further two years.

She is a Churchwarden at Holy Trinity Church and Treasurer of the 'Bungay In Bloom' Committee, being also involved in the W.V.S. Meals on Wheels scheme. A longstanding member of Bungay Tennis Club, she took an active part until recently.

Earlier in the year in which Mrs. Went was appointed Town Reeve, her son, Stephen, had become Town Mayor; no such situation had arisen before, and they represented Bungay together on a number of occasions. Mrs. Went was the tenth woman to be Town Reeve, and it was only the second time that one lady had directly succeeded another.

During her year of office, new paving was laid around the Butter Cross, and she attended the Waveney District St. George's Day parade in Bungay and the laying-up of the old Royal British Legion standard and the dedication of the new standard. As a result of the Bungay Festival, £800 was distributed to local organisations and £1,000 donated towards equipment for the new Bungay Medical Centre.

Mrs. Went became Mayor of Bungay in 2002, but resigned from the Town Council in 2007.

2000-01
ARTHUR WILLIAM FISHER

He was born on 12 November 1929 at All Hallows Hospital, Ditchingham, and educated at Ditchingham Primary School and Bungay Area School. He joined Richard Clay & Son in 1945, working for three years as an apprentice machine minder before undertaking two years of National Service in the Royal Artillery 71st Heavy Anti-Aircraft Regiment; he returned to Messrs. Clay in 1950. In the same year he joined Bungay St. John's Division as a volunteer driver, continuing to serve in this capacity for half a century. He was married in March 1953; he and his wife, Mavis, have three daughters.

In 1969 Mr. Fisher was elected the first full-time Secretary of the Waveney Towns Branch of the National Graphical Association, covering Beccles and Bungay, etc., and in 1974 he joined the Norfolk Ambulance Service, being stationed at Lowestoft and Beccles. He retired in November 1994.

Mr. Fisher was elected to Bungay Town Council for four years in 1970, and again in 1990, since when he has served continuously. He became Chairman in 1995 and Mayor in 1999; in the same year he was appointed Chairman of the Bungay Festival, and is also one of three Trustees of the Bungay Medical Centre.

Elected to the Town Trust as a Councillor Feoffee in 1992, he became the first Town Reeve of the New Millennium in 2000. The highlight of his year in office was the Remembrance Service at St. Edmundsbury Cathedral and Beating Retreat by the Coldstream Guards Band on the Angel Hill.

2001-02
Mrs. SUSAN VERA CURTIS

Miss Susan Cooke was born on 20 December 1961 in Great Yarmouth and lived at Aldeby, being educated at St. Benet's R.C. School in Beccles and St. Edmund's School in Gorleston, where she was Head Girl for two years. As a teenager she helped in a small market garden and in 1982 became a self-employed florist; she opened New Beginnings Florist in Earsham Street in 1995. The previous year she had married her second husband, Mr. John Curtis, in Las Vegas; she has two sons.

Having already been elected President of Bungay Chamber of Trade, Mrs. Curtis became a Town Councillor in 1999, serving for eight years. Appointed to the Town Trust as a Councillor Feoffee in 2000, the following year she became the eleventh woman Town Reeve, a few days before her 40th Birthday.

Early in her year of office, Mrs. Curtis had the sad duty of raising the Union Jack to half-mast on Bungay Castle on the occasions of the deaths of both H.R.H. the Princess Margaret and H.M. Queen Elizabeth the Queen Mother. However, later in the year she presided over Bungay's celebrations of the Golden Jubilee of H.M. Queen Elizabeth II (whom she met the following year as Deputy Town Reeve). In the summer of 2002 Mrs. Curtis held a large party at Bungay Community Centre, and was interviewed on stage as Guest of Honour at a Jubilee Conert held at Hunstanton. Approximately £1,500 was raised for various Bungay youth projects. To commemorate her year of office, Mrs. Curtis presented to the Town Trust a new gown and hat, to be worn by successive Town Reeves, replacing those donated in the 1950s, which are now on display in Bungay Museum (see p.93).

Mrs. Curtis became Mayor of Bungay in 2004, but resigned from the Council in 2007. In connection with their business, she and her husband are frequent visitors to the Netherlands.

2004-05
STEPHEN GLENN WENT

The son of Mrs. Roma Went (Town Reeve 1998-99), he was born on 18 August 1965 at Popson Street, Bungay, and educated at Bungay Primary, Middle and High Schools and Lowestoft College of Further Education, where he gained a B.E.C. Certificate in Business Studies. He has been employed by insurance brokers' firms, from 1983 to 2006 in Norwich and subsequently in Ipswich.

A single man, Mr. Went was elected to Bungay Town Council in 1995 and became Mayor in 1998, for six months of which his mother, Roma, was Town Reeve – three years later, she was also to serve as Mayor.

Mr. Went became a Councillor Feoffee in 1998, and was appointed Town Reeve in 2004 – the second time a son had followed a mother in office. He celebrated his 40th Birthday during his term of office by completing a 10,000 ft. tandem sky dive. During the year he also attended the official opening and dedication of the new Tower at Bury St. Edmunds Cathedral in the presence of T.R.H. the Prince of Wales and the Duchess of Cornwall. The 200th Anniversary of the Battle of Trafalgar was celebrated by a dinner and an anniversary concert by Bungay Choral Society at St. Mary's Church, and the new Skate Park was opened. The N.S.P.C.C. and Kids' Company benefitted by almost £2,000 through events held during the year.

An accomplished actor and a keen supporter of Norwich City Football Club, Mr. Went is closely involved with Holy Trinity Church, Bungay in Bloom and Bungay Theatre Group, and is a member of the Board of the Fisher Theatre.

2006-07
Mrs. MAUREEN DAVIES, B.A.

Miss Maureen Blyth was born on 12 February 1934 in Newcastle upon Tyne, and educated at Central Newcastle High School G.P.D.S.T. and King's College, Durham University. After graduation, she worked as a recruitment and training officer in Newcastle before marrying Mr. Michael Davies in 1959, having three children and moving abroad. She has lived in France, Switzerland, Belgium, the U.S.A. and South America, and came to Bungay in 1992.

Mrs. Davies has been Chairman of the Friends of All Hallows Hospital, a member of the Hospital Advisory Group, Chairman of the Bungay Reading Group and a member of the Committee of the Friends of St. Mary's Church. Appointed to the Town Trust as a Foundation Feoffee in 2005, she was nominated by Mrs. Mary Kent as the twelfth woman Town Reeve the following year; it was the third time that one lady had directly succeeded another.

During the Bungay Festival, Mrs. Davies hosted a Celebration of Anniversaries Dinner with the Mayor, and organised a garden party in the garden of her home, Rose Hall, which has been the home of several previous Town Reeves. The charities supported during Mrs. Davies's year of office were the Friends of All Hallows Hospital and Bungay in Bloom.

OFF WITH THE OLD, ON WITH THE NEW!

Mesdames Susan Curtis and Diana Belcher are pictured in Bungay Museum. Mrs. Belcher as Town Reeve is wearing the new gown and hat presented by Mrs. Curtis to commemorate her own year of office. The old gown, presented by Mr. John Clay (Town Reeve 1951-52), also seen here, is now on permanent display in the Museum.

ROYAL PROCLAMATIONS

It has traditionally fallen to the lot of the Town Reeve to proclaim in Bungay the Accession to the Throne of a new Sovereign.
All the Feoffees named below had already served, or were later to serve, as Town Reeve.

KING GEORGE VI
proclaimed Monday 14 December 1936

(Left to right) -, -, *R. E. Wightman, H. N. Rumsby,* -, *G. G. SPRAKE (TOWN REEVE), H. E. Bowerbank, A. C. Smith, Maj. W. H. Wortley, H. E. Rackham, E. H. Wightman,* -.

QUEEN ELIZABETH II
proclaimed Friday 8 February 1952

(Left to right) J. E. W. Gibbs, J. F. Keightley, Dr. L. B. Cane, -, -, D. L. Hewitt, -, R. J. Reynolds, G. G. Sprake, P. J. Sprake, R. E. Wightman, C. C. Rumsby, W. T. Courtney, -, C. B. Warnes, J. M. CLAY (TOWN REEVE), -, -, -, W. H. Sutton, Dr. L. H. Cane, -, -, -, C. H. Harris, -, Mrs. H. Nursey, Mrs. V. A. Stevens, -.

'THE TOWN REEVES OF BUNGAY'
(First Edition)
PRE-PUBLICATION RECEPTION
Friday 14 November 1986

The Town Reeve, Mrs. Cicely Smith, hands a copy of
'The Town Reeves of Bungay'
to the Senior Feoffee, Mrs. Rosalind Messenger.

John Harris signs a copy of his book for Mrs. Lilian Trafford
(twice Town Reeve), who was Headmistress of Bungay
Primary School throughout his time as a pupil there.

TOWN REEVES, 1986

The Town Reeve is pictured with her predecessors in office.
Back row (from l. to r.) :- Dr. Charles Maidment, Messrs. Colin Richardson, Harald Pulford, Jack Keightley, Richard Monks, Burton Nursey, Paul Woodcock, Dr. Wyndham Jordan.
Middle row (from l. to r.) :- Messrs. Tony Hood, Ivor Baldwin, Dr. Hugh Cane, Messrs. Michael Belcher, John Clay, Ron Duhy.
Front row (from l. to r.) :- Mr. Douglas Hewitt, Mesdames Mary Kent, Cicely Smith (TOWN REEVE), Rosalind Messenger, Lilian Trafford, Mr. John Gibbs.

THE ROYAL VISIT TO BUNGAY

On Wednesday 11 September 1991, Her Royal Highness The Princess Royal paid what is believed to be the first official royal visit to Bungay. In her capacity as President of the British Knitting and Clothing Export Council, Princess Anne spent part of the afternoon at the Upper Olland Street premises of Nursey & Son Ltd., in the year following their bicentenary celebrations.

The Princess Royal is welcomed to Bungay by the Town Reeve, Mr. Graham May, and his wife, Pat.

The Princess Royal talks to Mr. S. Burton Nursey (Town Reeve 1972-73) after unveiling a plaque commemorating her visit to his family's business premises.

REEVE MEETS MONARCH

The historic chain of office of the Town Reeve of Bungay was shown for the first time to a reigning Sovereign when Mr. Terry Reeve (Town Reeve 1996-97) met Her Majesty Queen Elizabeth II outside West Newton Parish Church, near Sandringham in West Norfolk, after morning service on Sunday 9 February 1997.

Her Majesty was interested to learn that commemorative royal medallions have been added over the years to the silver medal presented to Bungay Town Trust in 1820 to mark the Accession to the Throne of King George IV (see p.21); she also commented on the visit to Bungay made by her daughter, H.R.H. The Princess Royal, in 1991 (see p.98).

The Town Reeve told the Queen that he hoped she would be able to visit Bungay one day, to which Her Majesty replied that she would like to do so!

(Above) H.M. The Queen in animated conversation with the Town Reeve of Bungay, Mr Terry Reeve. (H.R.H. The Duke of Edinburgh can be seen in the background.)

(Right) Her Majesty admires the commemorative medal featuring Bungay Butter Cross, presented to her by Mrs. Carole Reeve.

MRS. TRAFFORD'S 100TH BIRTHDAY

The Senior Feoffee, Mrs. Lilian Trafford (twice Town Reeve), celebrated her 100th Birthday on Monday 1 March 2004. She is seen on the day at her home in Wharton Street, where she was visited by the Town Reeve and the Mayor, and by many friends and former pupils. Later in the week she was Guest of Honour at a Feoffees' Lunch hosted by the Town Reeve, and at a Reunion at Bungay Primary School, of which she was Headmistress, attended by approx. eighty of her former pupils.

Mrs. Trafford is greeted by the Town Reeve, Mrs. Diana Belcher, and the Mayor of Bungay, Mr. John Palin (Town Reeve 1987-88).

BUNGAY TOWN DINNER
Friday 1 December 2006

The Town Reeve and her personal guests are pictured before joining the assembled company at Bungay Community Centre.

From l. to r. : Mrs. Wendy Knowles, Mr. Les Knowles (Bungay Town Crier), Mrs. Pat Clarke, Mr. Tony Clarke, Mrs. Pauline Evans (Mayoress), Mr. Martin Evans (Mayor of Bungay), Mrs. Lyn Blizzard, Mr. Bob Blizzard (M.P. for Waveney), Mr. Stephen Went (Deputy Town Reeve), Mrs. Mary Kent (TOWN REEVE), Mr. John Harris, Mrs. Gwen Harris, Mr. Terry Reeve, Mrs. Penny Reeve, Rev. Bruce Waldron, Mrs. Sharn Waldron.

INDEX

The Town Reeves of Bungay 1725-2007 are listed in alphabetical order.

Abel, Matthias 24	Duhy, Ronald S. A. 67
Baldwin, Ivor G. 72	Fisher, Arthur W. 91
Barkway, Frederick 30	Fiske, Samuel 44
Bedingfield, James 38	Franklin, G. W. John 74
Belcher, Diana H. 84	Gamble, Dixon 19
Belcher, Michael P. 73	Garneys, Charles 30
Bellman, Henry 30	Gibbs, John E. W. 68
Botwright, John 15	Hancy, Colin R. 84
Botwright, Samuel 18	Harris, Cecil H. 66
Bowerbank, Hubert E. 49	Hartcup, Herbert J. 31
Brettell, John 24	Hartcup, William 30
Burtsal, Nelson 19	Haward, Edwin 32
Burtsal, Nelson 27	Hemblen, John 15
Burtsal, Robert (Snr.) 24	Hewitt, Douglas L. 54
Burtsal, Robert (Jnr.) 27	Hood, Anthony R. 68
Burtsal, Robert A. 27	Inwards, Horace J. 44
Butcher, Robert 27	Jervis, James H. 85
Camell, Robert 24	Jordan, Wyndham M. 72
Cane, Leonard B. 45	Keightley, Jack F. 63
Cane, L. Hugh 61	Kemp, John O. 38
Childs, Charles 31	Kent, Mary 74
Clarke, Robert 16	Kerrison, Edward 25
Clay, John M. 56	Kerrison, Matthias 20
Cocks, Alfred W. 39	King, James 14
Coe, Neville M. 62	King, John 14
Colborne, George 37	Kingsbury, Matthew B. 21
Cooper, Edward 17	Lamb, William 17
Cooper, John (Snr.) 19	Levick, Percy G. 61
Cooper, John (Jnr.) 25	Lewis, Wolfran 20
Courtney, William T. 56	Lockitt, Charles H. 43
Crockett, Douglas R. V. 74	Maidment, J. Charles H. 69
Curtis, Susan V. 91	Mann, John 27
Dalling, John (Snr.) 15	Mann, Richard (Snr.) 21
Dalling, John (Jnr.) 15	Mann, Richard (Jnr.) 27
Davies, Maureen 92	Mann, Robert C. 33
Denny, William 21	Mann, William 26

Manning, Thomas	17
Martin, Rosemary	80
May, Graham J.	81
McDaniel, Reginald G.	67
Meen, John	16
Messenger, Rosalind	50
Monks, Richard W. M.	75
Morrow, Peter	85
Nelson, Joshua	15
Nelson, Richard	14
Norman, William R.	39
Norton, Edmund P.	32
Nursey, Hilda	60
Nursey, S. Burton	72
Owles, H. Beaumont	36
Owles, Henry W.	33
Owles, Henry W.	55
Owles, Sidney J.	44
Palin, John V.	80
Parry-Crooke, Charles P.	48
Pell, William	18
Plowman, John W.	19
Plowman, Thomas	18
Prentice, Thomas	18
Pulford, Harald R. G.	78
Rackham, Herbert E.	45
Ramsbottom, Charles H. G.	37
Ransome, Gilbert H.	38
Reeve, Isaac	18
Reeve, Terence G.	87
Reynolds, Reginald J.	51
Richardson, D. Colin C.	78
Rumsby, Cecil C.	56
Rumsby, Harry N.	42
Scarle, Desmond P.	81
Scott, John	20
Scott, John B.	26
Scott, Peter D.	86
Sheppard, James	25
Smith, Austin C.	36
Smith, Cicely M.	79
Smith, Frederic	32
Smith, Samuel	31
Sprake, G. Guy	49
Sprake, Humphrey J.	42
Sprake, Percy J.	57
Sprake, Robert R. H.	51
Stevens, Vera A.	62
Sutton, Wilfred H.	60
Symns, James L. M.	42
Trafford, Lilian I.	66
Van Kamp, John	16
Walker, Pearse	26
Walker, Reginald H.	37
Walker, Thomas	16
Walker, William D.	33
Warnes, Betty J.	87
Warnes, Cecil B.	55
Went, Roma H.	90
Went, Stephen G.	92
Whyte, Herbert F.	69
Wightman, Ernest H.	36
Wightman, Frederick R.	39
Wightman, Henry	32
Wightman, Ronald E.	43
Williams, Henry	16
Williams, Robert	17
Woodcock, J. R. Paul	79
Wortley, Walter H.	63

BIBLIOGRAPHY AND SOURCES

Town Reeves' Books (accounts, minutes, etc.)
Town Reeves' Scrapbooks (press cuttings, etc.)
Old Bungay - Ethel Mann (1934)
An Englishman At Home And Abroad - J. B. Scott, ed. Ethel Mann
J. B. Scott Diaries 1829-1862, extracts
Bungay and District Guide - ed. Dr. Hugh Cane (1985)
Bungay Grammar School 1565-1965 - R. R. Houghton
Bungay Almanacs, 1888-1909
Kelly's Directories (several years)
White's Directories (several years)
Pigot Directory, 1839
Norfolk And Suffolk In The 20th Century (1911)
Cox's County Who's Who Series (1912)
Who's Who In Suffolk (1935)
East Anglian Pedigrees - ed. Campling (1940/45)
Norfolk And Norwich Portraits, Vol. 6 - Jacobson & Milne
Norfolk Families - W. Rye
Norfolk Genealogy, Vol. 6 - Palgrave-Moore & Sayer
Hunt & Co's East Norfolk (1850)
The Mayors of Norwich 1403-1835 - B. Cozens-Hardy & E. A. Kent (1938)
The Mayors And Lord Mayors of Norwich 1836-1974 - Patrick Palgrave-Moore (1978)
The Doors Of Opportunity - Rosalind Messenger (1967)
Clays of Bungay - James Moran (1978)
Wheel 'Em In, Bungay! - Terry Reeve (1985)
Waveney Valley - David R. Butcher (1975)
Old Bungay Records - H. J. Sprake (1906)
Reeves And Greaves - Dr. Leonard Cane
Three Centuries Of Bungay Doctors 1662-1978 - Dr. B. M. Goss
In Search Of The Kerrisons - Eric King
Holy Trinity Church, Bungay, Guide
Birth, Marriage & Death Records, St. Catherine's House, London
Parish Registers, Bungay (Suffolk Record Office, Ipswich)
Parish Registers, Norfolk Parishes (Norfolk Record Office, Norwich)
Census Returns, 1841, '51, '61, '71, '81 (S.R.O., Ipswich, & Norwich Library)
Ethel Mann Collection (Suffolk Record Office, Ipswich)
Bungay Obituary - M. B. Kingsbury
Wills (Suffolk Record Office, Ipswich)
Norwich Consistory Court Wills (Norfolk Record Office, Norwich)
Norfolk Poll Returns (various dates)
Tombstones & Memorials, St. Mary's & Holy Trinity Churches, Bungay - documented by Dr. Hugh Cane
Tombstones & Memorials, Bungay, Ditchingham, Hedenham & Thwaite
Press Cuttings, Eastern Counties Newspapers Library, Norwich
Eastern Daily Press (several years)
Beccles And Bungay Journal (several years)
Old Bungay News, Vol. I, no. 1 (18 June 1877)
Chaucer Press Review, Vol. VII, no. 1 (May 1952)
Various Documents, Bungay Museum
Various Documents, Colman Local History Library, Norwich
Questionnaires - Former Town Reeves and Relatives
Mrs. Messenger's Broadcast To America, 1938 (Script by Dr. L. B. Cane)
Charity Commission's Scheme For Bungay Town Trust (1984)
Notes - Mrs. Cicely Smith
Notes - Dr. Hugh Cane
Notes - Mrs. Rosalind Messenger
Notes - Mrs. Mary Kent
Notes - Mr. E. A. Goodwyn
Author's Memory!